THE SURREAL GOURMET

REAL FOOD FOR PRETEND CHEFS

Recipes and Illustrations by Bob Blumer

CHRONICLE BOOKS * SAN FRANCISCO

With love and respect for my mother,
who lived long enough to see me eat vegetables,
but not to see me write about them.

&

To my father who still chastises me
for using a bread knife to butter my toast.

Photography : Dick Kaiser
Design: Kevin Reagan
Edited by: Meesha Halm

Library of Congress Cataloging-in-Publication Data
Blumer, Bob.
the surreal gourmet: real food for pretend chefs / by Bob Blumer
p.   cm.
ISBN 0-8118-0121-7 (pb)
1. Cookery.   1. Title
TX714.B6   1992
641.5--dc20   91- 44419
                            CIP
Distributed in Canada by Raincoast Books,
112 East Third Avenue, Vancouver, B.C. V5T 1C8
10 9 8 7 6 5 4 3 2 1

Chronicle Books
275 Fifth Street
San Francisco, CA 94103

FOREWORD

BY JANE SIBERRY

bob is my manager.
bob is a best friend.
bob's cooking dinner tonight.

pull the stool around to the butcher block where i can see him working close-up. warm light here.

bob's kitchen is...a mysterious mixture of clean lines and thrown-to-the-wind, caricature and smudging. like his meals. like the way he presents them. like the way he annotates life. like a good cartoonist. drop out the filler, magnify the essence.

bob, perhaps you've forgotten to get the parmesan chunk for the caesar out of the fridge?

bob's kitchen is...everything is...hmmm...underlined. either by the lighting or the lack of clutter around it. not to say there isn't clutter here but...it's selective clutter. very bob and yet...how deep the imprinting on us all from the hours spent in the kitchen as children. hard as one tries, 99% of western civilization still ends up with the cutlery in the 1st drawer, the tea-towels and twist-ties in the 2nd. however, my mother would never have put a spotlight on the fridge. bob's selective clutter includes his collection of exotic condiments, spices, oils, vinegars. i like to investigate them the way i used to go through my mom's make-up.

can i turn down the music, bob?

next, pad over to the wine rack.

back on the stool. knees pointing stoveward.

ingredients start building on the butcher block. "bob is a selective being" i say as i settle back into the mood of musing. bob is a keeper of the gold. he has the ability to pan through the..."river of life?" she suggests hesitantly...and find the gold. to sift the special moments from a long stream of events and set them apart. underline them so that one says..."how did i not notice that before?" he is a collector of highlights. and so he is with cooking. all the details i read in his book spell luxury. in the best sense of the word. the kind of luxury available to everyone, not just kings. one would like to be poor with someone like bob.

ingredients continue building on the butcher block. bob chops it, i apologize to it, and then into the pan. we are a good team.

i am always amazed at bob's facility to cook and talk at the same time. sometimes explaining quite convoluted things as he does intricate...whatevers...cooking things. how radio formats work, independent promoters, mechanical royalties. things he has explained to me many times that i can never quite remember. probably because i can't listen and watch someone cook at the same time.

now bob's hands move into view. scooping up choppings like a man in prayer. and...there it is. i knew it would show up sooner or later. the cheese. old crumbly parmesan for the caesar salad. his feet recede. i'll just have a nibble. his feet reappear. i reach for the wine glass instead.

bob has a sixth sense about cheese. okay, so i nibbled all the parmesan for the salad one night by accident.

phone rings.

mmm. delicious. so sharp, so dusty, so precocious yet reticent.

okay bob i have just one comment for your book. grace. there should be a space for grace. that's all that i think is missing, otherwise i think it's wonderful. very rich. multi-level. and it has a lot of soul if one can say that about a cookbook or whatever kind of book this is. so...the idea of grace somehow. a moment of silence. a thank you to the moment.

phone rings.

INTRODUCTION

When Wolfgang Puck's literary agent called me to unceremoniously blow off our introductory meeting for the third and final time, he curtly inquired as to whether I was a professional chef. When I replied "no," he asked if I was a professional illustrator. When I replied "no," he responded, "Thank you, we have nothing more to discuss."

In my humble opinion, one need not be a professional chef to prepare gratifying food, or for that matter, to write about it. I believe that ignorance in the kitchen sweetens the taste of even the smallest culinary accomplishments. And for the uninitiated, those accomplishments need not remain small forever. With a little blind ambition, the culinary world can become your oyster.

Many of the pleasures of eating are not derived from the food itself, but rather from the comfortable atmosphere created around it. An evening dedicated to food should nourish all five senses: taste, touch, sight, smell, and sound. Fine dining establishments (if you can get a reservation and a bank loan) generally attempt to appeal to these senses, but only rarely will they attend to all of them. If and when they do, they usually undermine their best intentions by taking it all far too seriously. In the gleefully irreverent, shamelessly hedonistic world of *The Surreal Gourmet,* I attempt to invigorate all of the senses, and have a good time doing it.

The requirements for Surreal cooking are minimal. In my kitchen, the two most important tools undoubtably are the ancient butcher block upon which I prepare all of my food, and the well worn stools that overlook it. My friends perch on these stools, wine in hand, and we ease into the evening's chatter while I slice and dice.

As for hardware, all of my appliances are older than I am. They consist of an O'Keefe & Merrit gas stove, an International Harvester refrigerator, an original Osterizer blender, and a Hamilton Beach milkshake maker. No microwave, no food processor, no dishwasher, and no designer cookware.

My recipes are just as simple. Over the years, I have accumulated ideas from home, friends, and yes, restaurants, and stylized them to suit my individual tastes and patterns of entertaining. The essence of Surreal cooking takes common foods in their freshest state, assembles them into creative combinations, and brings them to life with the generous use of fresh herbs and spices. While some of the recipes expose my fondness for rich food, they reflect my personal philosophy that sumptuous dinners are the reward for working hard, exercising regularly, and eating a balanced diet. Virtually all the recipes here are designed to be prepared, from start to finish, in 30 minutes (not by coincidence, my pain threshold in the kitchen). The intent is to spend less time in the kitchen cooking and more time savoring the results and enjoying life. With this in mind, I have taken the liberty of interspersing amongst the recipes a collection of Surreal tips to help round out your cooking adventures.

As for the illustrations, they are simply an extension of the notion that food isn't only what it is, it's what you make it.

The whole package, I admit, is far from revolutionary. But on many occasions, in the midst of an evening of good cooking, in the company of friends and neighbors, I've had to pinch myself to confirm I hadn't died and gone to heaven. For me, this is what food is all about.

A USER'S GUIDE TO THE SURREAL GOURMET

This book is designed for modern food lovers who want to cook well with minimal effort and sacrifice. Unlike many cookbooks that present hundreds of recipes you'll never make, I have reduced the Surreal repertoire to a finely tuned collection of crowd pleasers that are relatively simple and quick to prepare. All of the recipes function well on their own or in combinations. Each one is accompanied by a list of suggestions to enhance the dish. If my suggestions happen not to suit your taste, use them as a springboard for inspiration to invent your own. Unseasoned cooks should skim through "The Art Of" and the "Staples" sections before firing up any burners. For those who can claim amateur chef status, skip these essentials and dive into the esoteric.

HEADINGS

LE SECRET: A key ingredient or step to be given extra attention.

THE ADVENTURE CLUB: If the sight of floating carrots didn't stop you from buying or receiving this book, you are a potential candidate for membership in The Adventure Club. The Adventure Club is a forum for presenting extra ingredients or twists that add additional dimensions to the recipe. Adventure Club members must be prepared to withstand fiery spices. They may be forced to drive great distances for uncommon ingredients, or spar with unaccommodating food store clerks. For those slightly less fervent about their food, the recipes survive quite nicely without these added adventures.

GARNISHES: Suggested garnishes, some standard, some surreal, to enhance the presentation.

SUGGESTED ACCOMPANIMENTS: Tried and true side dishes to complement each recipe.

ALTERNATIVES: A list of substitutions that have survived the Surreal Gourmet test kitchen. Do not allow yourself to be limited by these suggestions. Let common sense and your spirit of adventure be your guide. Mix and match the ingredients to suit your personal tastes and dietary quirks.

WINE: The wines suggested for each dish are intended to lead you away from your usual favorites and encourage experimentation, while remaining flexible where price or availability are concerned. For you learn-from-experience types, keep track of the wines you try in the journal at the back of the book. When shopping for wine, remember that the company, circumstance, and environment (notably, candlelight) can have more influence on your appreciation of a wine then the grapes it was squashed from. Don't let those wine snobs intimidate you.

MUSIC TO COOK BY: My suggestions for music to accompany your adventures in the kitchen are intended to feed and stimulate your aural senses. Each of the suggested albums is a classic. Because modern day commercial radio draws from such a limited pool of talent, you may be unfamiliar with some of these artists. For those interested in stretching their musical horizons, I have included an index with information about each of the recommended albums. Kick off your kitchen music collection by asking a dinner guest to bring the suggested album in place of wine. Almost all the recipes in *The Surreal Gourmet* can be prepared and cooked in approximately 30 minutes, which is just shy of the average length of the records I have suggested. Coincidence? I think not. This is the Surreal cooking's version of "musical chairs." Avoid being caught in the kitchen when the music ends.

SERVING SIZE: All the recipes are designed for two. To amend for one, three, or four people, simply proportion ingredients accordingly. For more than four, pause for a moment to consider the size of the utensils required and use common sense to alter portions. Fear not: unlike soufflés, none of these recipes collapse under the weight of misguided proportions.

A NOTE ON REDUCING BUTTER AND OIL: To reduce the cholesterol count of recipes requiring sautéing, replace butter with 1 tablespoon of a light vegetable oil (e.g., safflower oil). The recipes requiring olive oil will not suffer significantly if the amount of oil is reduced by one-third.

COOKING TO ORDER

Before cooking, I always ask my guest(s) to rate themselves on two sliding scales in order to adjust the ingredients to suit their tastes. These scales are as follows:

THE FEEDERMETER
On a scale of 1 - 10 (10 being the greatest), how hungry are you?

The entrée portions, when served with an accompaniment, should satisfy someone who hungers at the 7 level on the Feedermeter.

THE HEATERMETER
On a scale of 1 - 10, what is your pain threshold for the less subtle spices (i.e., garlic, onions, hot peppers)?

Throughout the book, I have preached what I practice in my kitchen. The exception to the rule is spicing. In real life, I am unabashedly heavy-handed when it comes to fresh herbs and spices. Still, even I bow to the wisdom of the Heatermeter, having watched more then one dinner guest spontaneously combust. I now realize that not everyone boasts the same spice tolerance. The proportions of herbs and spices in my recipes are intended to excite, but not overwhelm, the average palate. Use my Heatermeter to avoid disaster. Halve the spices listed in a given recipe for someone who is a 2. Use the recipe as it stands for someone who rates a 7. Double the spices for anyone who claims themself a 10.

THE READERMETER
The best ideas may be listed last. In order to score high on this scale, read through the entire recipe and accompanying suggestions before beginning to cook.

Recipes

ROASTED WHOLE GARLIC

(SERVES TWO)

The oyster of the '90s. Not just an appetizer but a culinary experience. The pine nuts, goat cheese, and Italian parsley act as a great foil to the pungent flavor of the roasted "stinking rose." Take one bite and go directly to garlic heaven!

INGREDIENTS
2 whole garlic bulbs*
6 tsp. olive oil
2 oz. strong goat cheese
I sourdough (preferable) or French baguette, *cut into 1/2" slices*
2 tbsp. roasted pine nuts (see Basics for roasting procedure)
6 sprigs of Italian parsley
I foot of tin foil

1) Slice 1/2" off the pointed end of the garlic bulb to expose each clove. Place garlic on the tin foil; pour one teaspoon of olive oil over the top of each bulb and let sink into the cloves. Wait 5 minutes and repeat twice.
2) Wrap foil around garlic bulbs along with the oil drippings so that it is sealed, and place on grill directly over hot charcoal BBQ for 25 minutes. (Grilling time may vary according to size of garlic bulb and flame.) Turn frequently. Two thirds of the way through grilling, poke a couple of fork holes in the tin foil to allow the charcoal flavor to permeate. (Be careful, escaping oil may cause flames to flare up.)
3) Toast bread ovals.
4) Divide goat cheese into two ovals.
5) Remove tin foil from garlic and artfully arrange the pine nuts, goat cheese, and parsley on plates around the garlic bulb.

To eat, extract individual garlic cloves from bulb with a small fork, spread on toast, and top with goat cheese, pine nuts, and parsley leaves.

LE SECRET: When cooked to perfection, cloves should be browned at the exposed end and soft throughout.
ADVENTURE CLUB: You're soaking in it!
GARNISH: Sprinkle ground black pepper around the outer edge of the plate.
SUGGESTED ACCOMPANIMENTS: This appetizer is self-contained.
ALTERNATIVES: Garlic may be baked in an oven instead of on the grill. (Place in pre-heated oven at 350 degrees for 60 minutes.)
NOTES: Garlic, like onions, becomes sweet when cooked. Consequently, eating a whole roasted garlic bulb is a completely different sensation from eating just one raw garlic clove. However, the next day you, and everyone around you, will still know you ate garlic. (But it will be well worth the commotion.)
MUSIC TO COOK BY: Jane Siberry, *Bound by the Beauty.*
WINE: An Alsatian Gewürztraminer [white].

* See the garlic section of Staple Spices for helpful information about garlic selection

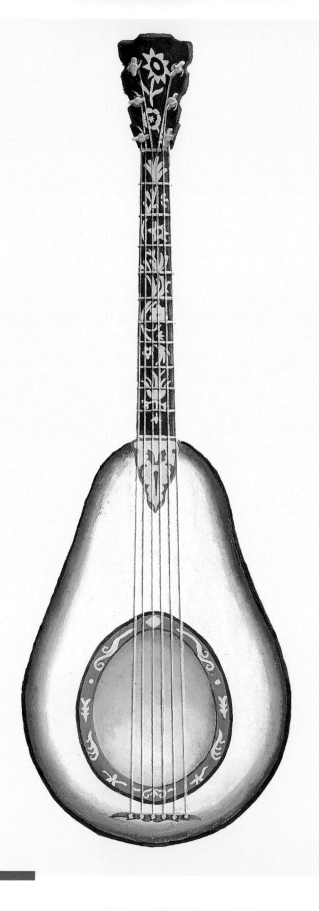

GUACAMOLE

(SERVES SIX TO EIGHT)
A spicier, fresher tasting variation of the traditional recipe.

INGREDIENTS
2 ripe avocados (Ripe = indents easily with the firm press of a finger...·
but don't let the produce person see you)
1/2 cup fresh cilantro, stems removed, *chopped finely*
1 dried hot red pepper, *crushed* (or 1 tsp. crushed chili peppers)
1 garlic clove, *minced*
Juice of 1 lemon
4 scallions, *chopped finely*
1 tsp. fresh ground black pepper, or to taste
1/2 tsp. salt, or to taste
1/8 tsp. cayenne pepper (optional)

1) Slice avocados in half, discard skin, and reserve pit.

2) In a bowl, add all ingredients. Blend with a fork or a double bladed chopper. (I prefer to leave my guacamole somewhat chunky.)

LE SECRET: At its best the day it is made. Only use ripe avocados and fresh cilantro.

ADVENTURE CLUB: Plant the avocado pit. Suspend the bottom half of the pit in a glass of water with toothpicks until it roots. Plant in garden or in a pot of soil.

GARNISH: Lemon twist.

SUGGESTED ACCOMPANIMENTS: Yellow or blue corn tortilla chips.

NOTES: (i) To keep "Guac" from turning brown, either squeeze the juice of 1/2 of a lemon over top or place avacado pit in the mixture. (ii) Use leftover guacamole in omelets, sandwiches, etc. (iii) Keep refrigerated.

ALTERNATIVES: Many people like to add a diced tomato.

MUSIC TO COOK BY: Los Lobos, *La Pistola y el Corazón.*

WINE: Sangria.

OLIVI PARADISO
(ITALIAN BLACK OLIVE PASTE)

(SERVES SIX TO EIGHT)

A guaranteed crowd pleaser that's certain to earn you sainthood in your own lifetime. This secret family recipe was divulged to me by an artful Italian friend. Share this with your friends *now* before the world catches on.

INGREDIENTS

2 cups of black Calamata olives (the smaller, thinner Greek ones)
2 cloves of garlic, *minced*
2/3 cup Italian parsley, *chopped*
5 large sprigs of fresh rosemary, *stems removed*
3 large sprigs fresh thyme, *stems removed*
1/3 cup olive oil
1 tsp. fresh ground black pepper

1) Pit the olives. Place olive between thumb and forefinger and squish. This takes a while but you will move quickly along the "learning curve." *
2) Place olives and all other ingredients in a blender or food processer and purée into a coarse mixture.

LE SECRET: Use good fresh Calamata olives** Err on the generous side of the herb portions.
ADVENTURE CLUB: Use olive paste on bruschetta (see Basics) or as a pizza base (see Stovetop Pizza).
GARNISH: Italian parsley.
SUGGESTED ACCOMPANIMENTS: Bagel chips or flavorful crackers.
ALTERNATIVES: Other types of black olives may be used, but at great sacrifice to the overall flavor.
NOTES: (i) Although no salt is added, the natural composition of Calamata olives makes this appetizer quite salty. (ii) If you are using a blender to purée, you may need to add some extra oil to facilitate blending. After blending, place in a bowl. Excess oil will rise to the edges of the bowl. Drain off. (iii) Keep refrigerated.
MUSIC TO COOK BY: Nino Rota, *Music from the Films of Fellini.*
WINE: Italian Chianti [red].

* The learning curve is a production management concept. It states that every time one doubles production (i.e., 2-4, 4-8, 8-16...), efficiency increases by 5%. In theory, since you will start at the beginning of the olive-pitting earning curve, your productivity will increase quickly.
** Calamata olives are difficult to find in grocery stores and overpriced in most delis. For the best olives at the lowest price, go to any Greek or Middle Eastern market.

GRILLED RUMANIAN EGGPLANT PURÉE

(SERVES SIX TO EIGHT)
This simple "Old World" recipe changes pedestrian eggplant into instant royalty.
Best described as a smoky cousin of Lebanese or Greek baba ghanouj.

INGREDIENTS
3 whole eggplants (the ones you used to buy before they "invented" Japanese eggplant)
1/2 cup olive oil
1 tsp. fresh ground coarse black pepper, or to taste
1 tsp. salt, or to taste

1) Place whole eggplants (unwrapped) on grill directly over a hot charcoal BBQ.
2) Rotate every 5 minutes until all of the skin is blackened to a crisp and eggplants have popped, blown steam
 like a kettle, and shrunken in size by approximately one third (approximately 30 minutes, depending on
 size and flame).
3) Remove from fire and let cool.
4) Remove skin and discard. Place remaining eggplant in a bowl.
5) By hand, chop finely.
6) Blend in oil, salt, and pepper.

LE SECRET: The key flavoring ingredient in this recipe is the grill. If possible, use real hardwood charcoal.
(Don't even *think* of cooking this in an oven.) Grill until totally blackened. The longer the eggplant cooks,
the more of the smoky grill flavor it absorbs.
ADVENTURE CLUB: Grill a couple hot peppers (i.e., jalapeno) along with the eggplant. Remove blackened
skin and slice in half to remove seeds. Chop finely and add to the eggplant.
GARNISH: Italian parsley.
SUGGESTED ACCOMPANIMENTS: Serve with triangles of toasted caraway rye bread or flavorful crackers.
NOTES: (i) Using a blender, instead of chopping, will purée the seeds which is undesirable.
(ii) If possible, prepare several hours before serving to allow flavors to blend. (iii) Keep refrigerated.
MUSIC TO COOK BY: The Gypsy Kings, *The Gypsy Kings*.
WINE: Greek Retsina [white]. Retsina is aged in pine, instead of the customary oak casks. While aging,
the wine inherits the flavor of the pine resin. The first sip tastes like turpentine, but you will warm up to
it after a couple of glasses. For Adventure Club members only!

CHEZ BOB'S CAESAR SALAD

(SERVES TWO AS A MEAL AND FOUR AS A SALAD COURSE)
Perfect this recipe and the world will beat a path to your door.

INGREDIENTS
1/2 tsp. salt
1 tsp. coarse ground black pepper
1 - 3 garlic cloves (depending on you and your guests' garlic threshold), *minced*
1 anchovy (or 1 tsp. anchovy paste)
1 tbsp. dijon mustard (the real stuff not the dried stuff)
1 egg yolk (Important: See Basics before using)
Juice of 1/2 lemon
1 tsp. Worcestershire sauce
1 tsp. red wine vinegar
1/3 cup vegetable (or olive) oil
1 medium-large head of romaine lettuce. *Discard outer leaves. Wash and dry remaining leaves thoroughly, then slice into bite-size pieces.*
1/3 cup grated parmesan cheese
1 cup croutons (purchase, or see Basics)

1) Into a large wooden salad bowl add ingredients up to the vinegar in order, one at a time.
2) After adding each new ingredient, use the back side of a soup spoon to blend it
with the previous ingredients into a smooth paste.
3) Add oil & vinegar and blend well.
4) *Just* before serving, add lettuce and toss thoroughly.
5) Add croutons and cheese, toss again, and serve.

LE SECRET: See The Art of the Salad.
ADVENTURE CLUB: Use imported Italian Reggiano Parmesan, grated just before using (the key to the definitive Caesar) and good croutons.
GARNISH: Top with an extra sprinkle of parmesan cheese.
SUGGESTED ACCOMPANIMENTS: This salad is complete on its own.
ALTERNATIVES: The anchovy is, of course, optional. I find that the flavor of olive oil overwhelms the dressing so I use safflower oil. However most back-seat chefs I know disagree. Mark Collis, a chef friend of mine from Toronto, eliminates the anchovy and adds a sun-dried tomato in oil which he blends into the paste.
NOTES: (i) Lettuce leaves should be coated, but not soaked, in dressing. (ii) Adjust amount of dressing for more or less lettuce to keep salad from becoming too "wet."
MUSIC TO COOK BY: Leonard Cohen, *I'm Your Man.*
WINE: A well chilled Australian Chardonnay [white].

*The Art of the Salad is suggested reading for anyone attempting "the definitive salad."

WARM WALNUT SALAD WITH ORANGE/ RASPBERRY DRESSING

(SERVES TWO AS A MEAL AND FOUR AS A SALAD COURSE)

A subtle combination of orange, walnut, and raspberry flavors, accentuated
with goat cheese. A perfect starter; flavorful, but not overwhelming.

INGREDIENTS

2 tsp. butter
1 leek, *sliced 1/4" crosswise and then washed*
1/2 cup walnuts, *whole or chopped*
2 oz. goat cheese, *cut or crumbled into 1/4" pieces*
1 head of butter lettuce
1 head of radicchio lettuce
3 tbsp. walnut oil
2 tbsp. raspberry vinegar
Zest of 1 orange, *grated finely* (just the orange part)
Salt and black pepper, to taste

1) Clean and dry butter lettuce and radicchio. Break into bite-size pieces and place in a salad bowl.
2) In a sauté pan, over med-high heat, melt butter.
3) Add leeks and sauté for 3 minutes, or until nicely browned.
4) Add walnuts and continue to sauté for 3 more minutes.
5) Remove pan from burner. Immediately add oil, vinegar, and orange zest to warm pan and let sit for
   20 seconds, or until thoroughly heated.
6) Top lettuce with goat cheese, salt, and pepper.
7) Pour contents of the pan over the goat cheese and lettuce. Toss thoroughly and serve.

LE SECRET: Toss thoroughly to warm evenly. The hot dressing is intended to warm the cheese and wilt the lettuce.
ADVENTURE CLUB: Try Roquefort or blue cheese in place of goat cheese.
GARNISH: Top with orange zest.
SUGGESTED ACCOMPANIMENTS: Serve as is for a salad course. As a meal, try adding a sliced, grilled
(or cooked otherwise) chicken breast or duck breast and orange slices with the peel removed.
ALTERNATIVES: Use Saladini or a mixture of other lettuces and/or fresh spinach. Replace walnuts with pine nuts.
MUSIC TO COOK BY: Van Morrison, *The Best of Van Morrison.*
WINE: Zinfandel blush.

CREAM OF BROCCOLI SOUP WITH WHITE WINE

(SERVES SIX TO EIGHT)

Most non-cooks assume that soup only comes from a can or a restaurant kitchen. Trust me, it's very simple and the end result is extremely gratifying. This particular recipe will make you an instant pro.

INGREDIENTS

Chicken or vegetable bouillon for 7 cups of stock
2 heads of broccoli, *lower portion of stems removed*
2 carrots, *peeled*
4 stalks of celery
1 large yellow cooking onion
1/4 lb. butter
1 cup of dry white wine (See Basics)
1 medium sized potato
4 tsp. dry oregano
1 tsp. dry thyme
1 tsp. salt
2 tsp. coarse black pepper
1 pint heavy cream

1) In a large pot, bring 7 cups of chicken or vegetable stock to a boil. Remove one cup and reserve.
2) Chop vegetables into small pieces. (Save one broccoli spear to use for garnish.)
3) In a sauté pan, melt half of the butter over med-high heat and sauté vegetables and herbs for approximately 15 minutes. Add remaining butter as needed.
4) Add wine, reduce heat to low, and let simmer for 5 minutes.
5) Add sautéed vegetables to stock, cover with a lid, and simmer for 30 minutes.
6) Allow soup to cool, and then purée in a blender.* Soup should have a thick and smooth consistency. After blending two thirds of the stock and vegetables, check the consistency of the blended soup. If it is too thin, drain off a cup of the remaining stock. If it is too thick, add the reserved cup of stock back into the pot. Continue to blend the remaining vegetables and stock.
7) Add salt and pepper.
8) To serve, add approximately 2 tbsp. of cream per serving and re-heat. Do not let boil.
9) Serve in warmed bowls.

LE SECRET: At its best when local broccoli is in season (look for a deep blue-green color).
ADVENTURE CLUB: Make your own stock.
GARNISH: Sprinkle with broccoli florets (fine pieces of broccoli top).
SUGGESTED ACCOMPANIMENTS: Fresh, thickly sliced, crusty bread.
ALTERNATIVES: Heavy cream may be substituted with half & half.
NOTES: (i) Vegetables may require two sauté pans. (ii) Adding the cream at the reheating stage, rather than all at once, extends the refrigerator life of the soup. (iii) If you plan to feed any vegetarians, use a vegetable stock.
MUSIC TO COOK BY: Nigel Kennedy, *Vivaldi's Four Seasons.*
WINE: California Riesling [white].

*__Warning:__ If you attempt to purée before soup has cooled down, the top of the blender will blow and you will have a green kitchen.

CREAM OF CARROT SOUP WITH FRESH GINGER

(SERVES SIX TO EIGHT)

A perfect fall or winter soup. Make it on a cold weekend afternoon and let the wafting smell of the ginger
and nutmeg and the heat of the simmering stock pot warm your entire house.

INGREDIENTS

Chicken or vegetable bouillon for 7 cups of stock
2 lbs. fresh carrots, *peeled*
3 leeks, *sliced in half lengthwise and thoroughly cleaned*
1 yam (sweet potato)
4 stalks of celery
3" piece of fresh ginger root, *peeled and grated*
1/4 lb. butter
1 tsp. salt
1 tsp. black pepper
1 tsp. ground nutmeg
1 pint of heavy cream

1) In a large pot, bring 7 cups of chicken or vegetable stock to a boil. Remove 1 cup and reserve.
2) Chop all vegetables into small pieces.
3) In a sauté pan, over med-high heat, melt half of the butter. Sauté vegetables with ginger and nutmeg for
   approximately 15 minutes, until vegetables are all browned. Add remaining butter as needed.
4) Add sautéed vegetables to stock, reduce heat, cover with a lid, and simmer for 30 minutes.
5) Let cool to room temperature and then purée in a blender.* Soup should be thick and smooth. After blending
   two thirds of the stock and vegetables, check the consistency of the blended soup. If it is too thin, drain off a cup
   of the remaining stock. If it is too thick, add the reserved cup of stock back into the pot. Continue to blend the
   remaining vegetables and stock.
6) Add salt and pepper.
7) To serve, add approximately 2 tbsp. of cream per serving and re-heat. Do not let it boil.
8) Serve in warmed bowls.

LE SECRET: Taking the time to brown the vegetables before simmering them brings out their naturally
sweet flavors. The browner (without burning), the better.
ADVENTURE CLUB: Make your own stock. (See Basics.)
GARNISH: Float a small piece of the carrot top greenery in the center of the bowl.
SUGGESTED ACCOMPANIMENTS: A warm loaf of multi-grain bread.
NOTES: (i) Vegetables may require two pans. (ii) Adding the cream at the reheating stage, rather than all at once,
extends the refrigerator life of the soup. (iii) If you plan to feed any vegetarians, use a vegetable stock.
ALTERNATIVES: Use half & half instead of heavy cream.
MUSIC TO COOK BY: The Neville Brothers, *Yellow Moon.*
WINE: French Beaujolais [red].

Warning: If you attempt to purée soup before it has cooled down, the top of the blender will blow and you will have an
orange kitchen! (Trust me, I've been there.)

CREAM OF PESTO PASTA WITH ASPARAGUS & CORN

(SERVES TWO)

An excellent first recipe to try from this book. It's simple to prepare, visually pleasing, and very tasty.

INGREDIENTS

1/4 tsp. salt

4 tbsp. butter

1 fresh ear of corn, *husk and remove kernels with a sharp knife. Discard cob (or save to make a pipe)*

10 spears of asparagus, *discard bottom quarter of spear and cut remainder into 1" pieces*

1 - 2 garlic cloves, *minced*

1 fresh or dried hot pepper, *finely diced or crushed* (very optional)

2 servings of fresh Angel hair egg pasta (approximately 4 oz./serving)

1/3 cup half & half cream

4 tbsp. (3 oz.) fresh pesto sauce (purchase or see Basics)

1/3 cup of grated parmesan cheese

1/2 tsp. fresh ground black pepper

1) In a large pot, bring 6 cups of salted water to a boil.
2) In a sauté pan, over med-high heat, melt 2 tbsp. butter. Sauté asparagus, corn, garlic, and hot pepper for 5 - 8 minutes until corn kernels begin to brown. Reserve in a warmed bowl. Save pan for step 4.
3) Add pasta to boiling water and cook according to directions.
4) In the same sauté pan, over low heat, melt remaining 2 tbsp. butter and slowly stir in cream, parmesan (save a pinch for the garnish), pesto, and black pepper. Stir and allow to simmer over lowest heat for 2 minutes.
5) Drain pasta.
6) Add pasta to pesto cream sauce (already in pan). Toss.
7) Serve on warmed plates or bowls. Top with asparagus and corn.

LE SECRET: Use good pesto.

ADVENTURE CLUB: Make your own pesto (see Basics).

GARNISH: A basil leaf and a sprinkle of parmesan.

SUGGESTED ACCOMPANIMENTS: Serve with fresh, crusty bread.

ALTERNATIVES: Fresh Angel hair pasta can be replaced with any other shape and form of pasta. An equal amount of plain yogurt may be substituted for the cream with minimal sacrifice. Fresh corn may be replaced with 2/3 cup of frozen baby corn kernels (thawed). Substitute asparagus with something creative when it is out of season.

MUSIC TO COOK BY: Louis Prima, *Zuma*.

WINE: Burgundy [red or white].

CAJUN FUSILLI PASTA

(SERVES TWO)

If Paul Prudhomme and Luciano Pavarotti were twins separated at birth, this is probably
what their mother would have cooked.

INGREDIENTS

1 yam, *sliced and diced into 1/4" cubes*
1/4 tsp. salt
4 tbsp. butter
1 yellow summer squash, *cut into 1/4" slices*
1 chicken breast, *skinned, boned, and sliced into 3/4" cubes* (purchase preboned or see Basics)
1/2 cup fresh dill, *stems removed and chopped coarsely*
2 servings of fusilli pasta (approx. 2 oz. per serving, dry, 4 oz. fresh)
1/3 cup half & half cream
1/3 cup grated parmesan cheese
2 tsp. Cajun spices (purchase premixed or see Basics)

1) Steam yam for 10 minutes (See Basics).
2) In a large pot, bring 6 cups of salted water to a boil.
3) In a sauté pan over med-high heat, melt 2 tbsp. of butter and sauté yam until slightly browned.
   Add chicken, squash, and dill (save a bit for the garnish) and sauté until chicken pieces are cooked
   throughout. Reserve in a warmed bowl. Save pan for step 5.
4) Add pasta to boiling water and cook according to directions.
5) In the same sauté pan, over low heat, melt remaining 2 tbsp. of butter and slowly stir in cream and
   parmesan (save a bit to sprinkle over completed meal). Add Cajun spices and simmer over
   low heat for two minutes.
6) Drain pasta. Add pasta to cream sauce (already in pan). Toss.
7) Serve on warmed plates or bowls. Top with sautéed ingredients.

LE SECRET: The spices make the sauce. If you are purchasing a premix, make sure the variety you
buy includes most of the ingredients listed in Basics.
ADVENTURE CLUB: Replace chicken with fresh crayfish.
GARNISH: Sprinkle with dill and parmesan.
SUGGESTED ACCOMPANIMENTS: Fresh, crusty bread.
ALTERNATIVES: An equal amount of plain yogurt may be substituted for the cream with
minimal sacrifice. Replace yellow squash with other seasonal vegetables.
MUSIC TO COOK BY: Boozo Chavis, *Boozo Chavis*.
WINE: Spanish Rioja [red].

CALIFORNIA CARBONARA

(SERVES TWO)
A California kitchen sink version of the classic Italian pasta.

INGREDIENTS
1/4 tsp. salt
4 - 6 strips of bacon, and/or pre-cooked BBQ chicken breast *(diced)*
6 shallots or 1 leek, *sliced crosswise 1/4" and washed thoroughly*
1 - 2 garlic cloves, *minced*
1 fresh or dried hot pepper, *diced (optional)*
6 sun-dried tomatoes (marinated in oil), *sliced thinly*
2 tbsp. pine nuts
1/2 cup grated parmesan cheese
2 eggs (Important: See Basics before using)
1/2 cup half & half cream
1 tsp. fresh ground black pepper
2 servings of fresh Angel hair, egg, or spinach pasta (approximately 4 oz./serving)
1/4 cup Italian parsley, *stems removed and chopped*
Any fresh: **basil, thyme, rosemary, oregano, savory,** *stems removed,* to taste (optional)

1) In a large pot, bring 6 cups of salted water to a boil.
2) In a frying pan over med-high heat, cook bacon to medium crispness. Once cooked, drain fat and chop into 1/2" slices. Reserve.
3) Over med-high heat melt butter in a sauté pan. Add shallots (or leek), garlic, hot peppers, and pine nuts and sauté for 5 minutes or until browned.
4) Add pasta to boiling water and cook according to directions.
5) Reduce heat of sauté pan to med-low and add sun-dried tomatoes, bacon, fresh herbs (other than parsley), and pre-cooked chicken (optional) for 2 minutes.
6) In a bowl, beat eggs, cream, black pepper, and all but 1 tbsp. of the cheese.
7) Remove sauté pan from burner and leave contents in pan.
8) Drain pasta, then place in sauté pan.
9) Pour egg mixture over pasta and sautéed contents. Add parsley. Toss for about 30 seconds allowing the egg mixture to thoroughly coat the pasta.
10) Serve on warmed plates or bowls.

LE SECRET: The heat of the pasta lightly cooks the egg mixture. Execute steps 8 & 9 as quickly as possible.
ADVENTURE CLUB: Try one of the proliferating species of unusually flavored pastas (lemon/pepper, tomato/basil, etc.)
GARNISH: Three leek slices, 1/4", cut crosswise at a 45 degree angle, placed side by side, and a sprinkle of parmesan.
SUGGESTED ACCOMPANIMENTS: Serve with crusty Italian bread.
ALTERNATIVES: Fresh Angel hair pasta can be replaced with any other shape or form of pasta. Replace bacon with sliced prosciutto.
MUSIC TO COOK BY: Various artists, *Legends of Guitar, Surf Vol. 1.*
WINE: Italian Barolo [red].

GLAZED ITALIAN CHICKEN

(SERVES TWO)
A quick and sumptuous way to prepare a boneless chicken breast.

INGREDIENTS
2 chicken breasts, *boned and skinned with tendons removed* (buy pre-boned or see Basics)
1/4 tsp. salt
1/4 tsp. black pepper
1/4 cup flour
1 egg
1/2 cup coarse bread crumbs (purchase or see Basics)
1/4 cup grated parmesan cheese
2 sprigs fresh oregano, *stems removed,* or 1 tbsp. dry oregano
2 sprigs fresh thyme, *stems removed,* or 1 tbsp. dry thyme
3 tbsp. butter
2 lemons, *1 juiced, 1 sliced*

1) Rinse chicken and pat dry.
2) Place chicken between 2 sheets of wax paper or a suitable alternative, and pound with a mallet until 1/4" thin: sprinkle with salt and pepper.
3) In three separate bowls place: (bowl #1) flour, (bowl #2) egg (beaten), and (bowl #3) bread crumbs, cheese, and herbs mixed. Line the three bowls in a row.
4) Take chicken breasts, roll in flour, dip in egg until well soaked, and then roll in bread crumb mixture until well covered.
5) In a sauté pan, over med-high heat, melt half of the butter. Add breaded chicken when pan is very hot.
6) Sauté until golden brown. Turn only once. (It should take 2 - 3 minutes on each side, depending on exact thickness.)
7) Remove chicken from pan and place on warmed plates.
8) Add remaining half of butter and lemon juice to drippings. Stir for a few seconds and then pour over the chicken.
9) Serve on warmed plates.

LE SECRET: The trick is to brown the outside of the chicken, cook it thoughout, and still keep the meat moist. Needless to say, it's all in the timing. Make a small incision in the middle when you think it is almost done. It's cooked to perfection just after all of the pink is gone.
ADVENTURE CLUB: Serve Grappa (an Italian *eau-de-vie*) after dinner.
GARNISH: Lemon twist.
SUGGESTED ACCOMPANIMENTS: Serve with brown sugar carrots. Add peeled sliced or whole baby carrots and 4 tbsp. brown sugar to 4 cups of water. Boil for 20 minutes, remove, and glaze with butter.
ALTERNATIVES: Substitute chicken with veal.
MUSIC TO COOK BY: Various artists, *Puccini's Greatest Hits.*
WINE: Italian Chardonnay from Tuscany [white].

34

CHICKEN KIEV ('90s VERSION)

(SERVES TWO)

This recipe for Chicken Kiev mirrors today's Soviet Union. The original shell remains the same but the inner workings have been revamped. Well suited for entertaining as it can be prepped hours in advance (keep refrigerated).

INGREDIENTS

4 strips of bacon
2 large chicken breasts, *boned, skinned, and tendons removed* (buy pre-boned or see Basics)
I egg
1/2 cup of bread crumbs (coarse if possible)
1/4 cup flour
3 sprigs of fresh thyme, *stems removed* or 1 tbsp. dry thyme
2 sprigs of Italian parsley, *stems removed and chopped*
6 asparagus tips (top 2" only)
2 tbsp. butter
I orange, *cut into 1/4" slices*

1) Pre-heat oven to 350 degrees.
2) In a frying pan, cook bacon until almost crispy.
3) Steam asparagus tips for three minutes (See Basics).
4) Using a mallet, or other blunt instrument (the kind you keep beside your bed to ward off mad burglars), flatten chicken breasts by placing them, one at a time, between 2 sheets of wax paper or a suitable alternative, and pound to 1/4" thickness.
5) In three separate bowls place: (bowl #1) flour, (bowl #2) egg (beaten), and (bowl #3) bread crumbs and thyme, mixed. Line the three bowls in a row.

Complete the following procedure for each serving:
6) Take one flattened chicken breast, sprinkle with salt, pepper, and chopped parsley.
7) Lay two strips of bacon side by side, on the top side of the chicken breast. Place three asparagus tips crosswise at one end and top with 1 tbsp. butter.
8) Starting at the end with the asparagus, roll up chicken like a carpet around the bacon, butter, and asparagus, and tuck in the loose ends underneath.
9) Dip chicken roll in the flour, then the egg, and then the bread crumbs, covering thoroughly at each step.
10) Place in a shallow pan with the seam on the bottom and bake for 15 - 20 minutes. Towards the end, baste with pan drippings.
11) Serve on warmed plates.

LE SECRET: To maintain moistness and prevent butter leakage during cooking, wrap chicken around ingredients carefully, creating as airtight a pocket as possible.
ADVENTURE CLUB: Invent your own center filling.
GARNISH: Orange twist.
SUGGESTED ACCOMPANIMENTS: I serve the chicken on a nest of wild rice. (Uncle Ben's Long Grain & Wild Rice is the simplest short cut to easy wild rice.)
ALTERNATIVES: Replace asparagus and bacon center with prosciutto and flavorful cheeses (e.g., blue cheese), or a mixture of 2 cups fresh spinach, steamed for 2 minutes and then sautéed for 2 minutes in 1 tbsp. butter with 2 oz. of crumbled feta cheese.
MUSIC TO COOK BY: The Bulgarian State Female Vocal Choir, *Le Mystère des Voix Bulgares*.
WINE: Dry Alsacian Riesling [white]. Adventure Club members should chase with shots of Stoli vodka.

STEAK AU POIVRE

(SERVES TWO)

In this day of red meat consciousness, this is a delicious way to enjoy a small, delicate portion of steak.

INGREDIENTS
2 tsp. fresh ground black pepper, *ground coarsely*
1/4 tsp. salt
1 tbsp. butter*
2 tenderloin steaks: 6 oz. each, 3/4" thick
3 tbsp. Cognac (1 1/2 oz.)
2 tsp. Dijon mustard
1/2 cup half & half cream
2 sprigs watercress

1) Rub salt and ground black pepper over both sides of the steak.
2) In a sauté pan melt butter over high heat. When pan becomes very hot add steaks. Turn only once and cook to desired degree of wellness. (Approximately 3 minutes per side for medium-rare, depending on exact thickness.)
3) Add Cognac to pan, let sit for five seconds and then light a match to it.** Flame should burn out after approximately 10 seconds. If flame continues to burn, put it out by placing a lid on the pan.
4) Remove steak from pan (leaving drippings in the pan) and reserve on a warm plate.
5) Reduce heat to low and slowly stir cream and Dijon into the drippings. Stir and simmer for a couple of minutes until sauce gains some thickness.
6) Place steaks on warmed serving plates.
7) Pour sauce over steak.

LE SECRET: The high heat will cook this delicate cut of steak fairly quickly. To avoid overcooking, make an incision in the middle of the steak to check the color.
ADVENTURE CLUB: Add 2 tbsp. of canned green peppercorns in step 5 (highly recommended).
GARNISH: Sprig of watercress.
SUGGESTED ACCOMPANIMENTS: Steamed whole green beans glazed with lemon and butter.
ALTERNATIVES: This sauce will work well with most cuts of steak.
NOTES: (i) Be prepared, this particular cut of steak is expensive, but worth it. (ii) Be careful when flambéing. The flame will jump 2 - 3 feet high as soon as the match touches the Cognac. (iii) Most of the alcohol content of the Cognac burns off during flambéing.
MUSIC TO COOK BY: Lyle Lovett (he's from Texas), *Pontiac*.
WINE: California Cabernet Sauvignon or French Bordeaux [red].

* This is a good recipe to experiment with clarified butter (see Basics).
** For those without fire insurance, skip the flambéing action and add 2 tbsp. Cognac along with the cream in step 5.

SALMON GRILLED BETWEEN
ROMAINE LETTUCE LEAVES

(SERVES TWO)

This is one of my favorite recipes in this book. The presentation value and taste sensation are truly greater than the sum of its parts. Well suited for entertaining since it can be prepped hours in advance. (Keep refrigerated.)

INGREDIENTS

4 large romaine lettuce leaves
6 tsp. olive oil
2   1" thick salmon steaks or salmon fillets, approximately 6 oz. each
Salt & pepper, to taste
2 tbsp. capers
4 sprigs of fresh dill
2 lemons, *1 juiced, 1 sliced thinly*
2 pieces of twine: 3 ft. each (or other nonflammable natural fiber)

1) Soak twine in hot water for 15 minutes.
2) Rinse salmon in cold water and pat dry with towel.
   Repeat the following for each salmon steak
3) Rinse romaine leaves in water, do not dry. Rub 1 tsp. of the oil over the inside (concave) side of each of the lettuce leaves.
4) Place salmon steak in center of one leaf (concave side up).
5) Add salt and pepper.
6) Pour 1 tsp. oil and the juice of 1/2 lemon over salmon, trapping the drippings with the leaf.
7) Top with capers, dill, and one lemon slice.
8) Place second leaf over salmon, fold ends of bottom leaf up to keep juices trapped, and wrap the string around the leaves to seal. Tie string in a knot (see Basics for illustration).
9) Place fish on grill over hot coals for 5 minutes. Turn and grill for another 5 minutes. Cooking time will be slightly less for fillets and will vary according to the exact thickness of the steak.
10) Cut string and remove top leaf. (You may want to leave string on for presentation value.) Serve on warmed plates.

LE SECRET: Do not overcook the salmon. To test, make an incision in the middle. Tastes vary, but most people like their salmon a light pink with just a faint hint of red in the very center.
ADVENTURE CLUB: Go catch the salmon yourself.
GARNISH: Blackened bottom romaine leaf and a lemon twist.
SUGGESTED ACCOMPANIMENTS: Serve with your choice of grilled vegetables (see Grilled Vegetables).
NOTES: (i) Keep track of which end is the top (with capers and dill) when removing leaf to serve.
(ii) Don't buy salmon steaks that are bigger than the romaine leaves. (iii) The grilled lettuce is good to eat.
(iv) Even though salmon is a bit pricey, the small serving size keeps it affordable, even for large dinner parties.
ALTERNATIVES: This may also be cooked under a pre-heated broiler for 5 minutes per side.
MUSIC TO COOK BY: Ella Fitzgerald and Louis Armstrong, *Porgy and Bess.*
WINE: French Burgundy [white].

SHRIMP SAUTÉED WITH FENNEL & PERNOD

(SERVES TWO)
Most shrimp never had it this good.

INGREDIENTS
1 lb. large or jumbo-sized shrimp, *shelled and deveined*
3 tbsp. butter
1/2 fresh fennel bulb
2 1/2 oz. Pernod (an alcohol)
Juice of 2 lemons
20 chives, *chopped*
1/2 cup white wine
Salt and ground black pepper, to taste

1) Peel the shrimp by removing the shells. (Leave tail flange on if you like.) To devein, make a shallow cut along the back of the shrimp and remove the dark intestinal vein that runs along the back.
2) Cut fennel bulb in half, core out center and discard (but save the dill-like tops for garnish). Slice remaining bulb thinly.
3) In a sauté pan over med-high heat, melt 1 tbsp. butter.
4) Add fennel and sauté for 5 minutes.
5) Melt additional 2 tbsp. butter in pan and add shrimp. Sauté shrimp until pink (approximately 1 - 2 minutes, depending on size).
6) Add Pernod to pan, let sit for five seconds and then light a match to it.* Flame should burn out after approximately 10 seconds. If it continues to burn, put it out by placing a lid on the pan. Remove shrimp and reserve.
7) Add chives, lemon juice, wine, salt, and pepper. Reduce heat to medium for 2 minutes and allow liquids to thicken slightly.
8) Return shrimp to pan for 1 minute.
9) Serve on warmed plates.

LE SECRET: In order to avoid overcooking the shrimp, slightly undercook them in step 5. They will finish cooking in step 8.
ADVENTURE CLUB: Cut decorative carrot flowers to enhance presentation.**
GARNISH: Sprinkle with small pieces of fennel top.
SUGGESTED ACCOMPANIMENTS: Serve over white rice flavored with fish stock and diced chives.
ALTERNATIVES: Wild rice or other flavored rices.
NOTES: (i) Cooking time of shrimp will vary according to size. (ii) Be careful when flambéing. The flame will jump 2 - 3 feet high as soon as the match touches the Pernod. (iii) Most of the alcohol content of the Pernod burns off during flambéing.
MUSIC TO COOK BY: Edith Piaf, *The Voice of the Sparrow*.
WINE: French Chablis [white].

*For those without fire insurance, skip the flambéing action and stir in 3/4 oz. of Pernod after step 7 when pan has been removed from heat and is away from all flames.
** Peel one medium sized carrot. Cut off top and bottom. Using the round end of a common vegetable peeler, dig 5 evenly spaced 1/4" grooves down the entire length of the carrot. Slice crosswise in 1/8" pieces. Add in step 7. If you are willing to go the extra mile, some Asian restaurant supply stores sell flower and animal shaped molds for this purpose.

SCALLOPS TROPICANA

(SERVES TWO)

Instructions for an instant tropical vacation: 1) Turn up the thermostat.
2) Put Jimmy Cliff on the stereo. 3) Blend yourself a daiquiri. 4) Follow the recipe.

INGREDIENTS

1 lb. fresh scallops
Juice of 3 limes
2 tbsp. butter
1 ripe banana, *peeled and sliced into 1/4" slices*
1/2 mango, *peeled, pitted, and sliced lengthwise into 1/2" strips*
2/3 cup coconut milk (not to be confused with coconut cream)
1/3 tsp. cayenne pepper
3 tbsp. shredded coconut
4 scallions, *sliced finely*
4 tbsp. fresh cilantro, *stems removed, chopped*

1) Remove the tough muscle on the side of the scallops (most stores will have already done this for you).
2) Marinate scallops in juice of 2 limes for 15 minutes.
3) In a sauté pan over high heat, melt 1 tbsp. butter and sautée scallops for approximately 1 minute per side or until you see a hint of brown on the outside.
4) Remove and reserve in a warmed bowl.
5) Reduce heat to medium and add remaining tbsp. of butter. Sauté banana, mango, scallions, and 2 tbsp. of shredded coconut for 3 minutes.
6) Add coconut milk, the remaining lime juice, and cayenne pepper; reduce heat and let sauce thicken slightly for 2 minutes.
7) Return scallops to sauce, add 2 tbsp. cilantro, and simmer for 2 more minutes.
8) Serve on warmed plates.

LE SECRET: Don't overcook the scallops.
ADVENTURE CLUB: Buy a real coconut and use its milk and meat in place of the canned milk and shredded coconut.* This is lots of fun; it improves the flavor and it's even economical. Most grocery stores carry coconuts.
GARNISH: Sprinkle with remaining shredded coconut and cilantro.
SUGGESTED ACCOMPANIMENTS: Serve over cous cous (highly recommended) or white rice.
ALTERNATIVES: Sliced boneless chicken or escargot may be substituted for scallops.
MUSIC TO COOK BY: Jimmy Cliff, *The Harder They Come* (Soundtrack).
WINE: Dry Sauvignon Blanc [white].

* Pierce the softest of the three tiny holes at the top of the coconut. Drain the milk into a bowl (this is technically "coconut water," but it works perfectly for this recipe). Break open the coconut with a hammer and remove the white coconut meat. Remove the brown outer layer with a vegetable peeler. Grate the meat with a coarse grater.

BUILD YOUR OWN STOVETOP GOURMET PIZZA

(SERVES ONE)

The recent surge in popularity and availability of fresh, flat, round, Italian-style breads* makes the preparation of homemade gourmet pizza a snap. I developed the start-to-finish-in-10-minutes-no-fuss-no-muss-stovetop-method when my oven was broken and I've never looked back. Assemble your own list of ingredients, or try one of my two favorite combinations.

INGREDIENTS

1 tbsp. butter
1 tbsp. vegetable oil
6" pizza bread
Selected toppings
Fresh or dried herbs, to taste
1/4 cup selected tomato sauce, purée, or pesto
2 oz. of selected cheese, *cut into 1/4" cubes*

Suggested combinations:

PIZZA #1: 4 sun-dried tomatoes, *sliced,* 1/4 leek, *sliced crosswise in 1/4" slices and washed,* 1 tbsp. pine nuts, 2 oz. wedge of brie cheese *cut into 1/4" cubes,* 1/2 of a small pre-cooked BBQ'd chicken breast, *sliced,* 3 tbsp. pesto sauce (purchase or see Basics), 6" pizza shell

PIZZA #2: 2 scallions, *sliced thinly,* 2 marinated artichoke hearts, *quartered,* 1 pinch of oregano, 2 oz. of goat or feta cheese, black olive purée** (see Olivi Paradiso recipe), 6" pizza shell

1) In a sauté pan, over medium heat, melt butter. Sauté uncooked toppings for 3 minutes. Add pre-cooked ingredients and herbs and continue to sauté for 2 more minutes.
2) Remove contents from pan and reserve in a warm bowl.
3) Add vegetable oil to pan and increase heat to med-high.
4) Place pizza bread in pan and brown on one side for 2 minutes.
5) Turn over, reduce heat to low, and spread pesto, olive paste, or tomato sauce on the top cooked side of pizza bread.
6) Place all topping ingredients over the sauce and sprinkle with cheese.
7) Cover tightly for 2 - 3 minutes, or until cheese melts.
8) Serve on a warmed plate.

LE SECRET: Don't be restricted by what "should" go on the pizza.
ADVENTURE CLUB: Mix and match. Try any or all of the following: asparagus, chopped peppers, fancy sausages, broccoli, exotic mushrooms, capers, raw or grilled sweet peppers, tomatoes, sun-dried tomatoes, garlic, garden herbs, and various cheeses.
GARNISH: The pizzas are self-garnishing.
SUGGESTED ACCOMPANIMENTS: Perfect with Caesar Salad.
ALTERNATIVES: Can be baked in oven. Replace step 7 by broiling for 2 minutes. This alternative is required for larger sized pizza breads.
MUSIC TO COOK BY: Tom Waits, *Frank's Wild Years.*
WINE: Experiment with various imported beers.

* My favorite brand is called: Boboli (no relationship). Available at most supermarkets.
** As an alternative to black olive purée, cut up a few olives and add to the toppings. In this case use a tomato sauce as a base.

GRILLED VEGETABLES

One of the easiest, yet most flavorful methods of preparing vegetables.
Grilled veggies are a perfect addition to any meat, fish, or chicken dinner, grilled
on the BBQ, or as a meal itself. Ideal when local produce is in season.

Try any combination of the following:

Corn, *as is, in its husk*
Yam, *skin on, sliced 1/2" thick and steamed for 10 minutes (see Basics)*
Baby new potatoes, *skin on, steamed for 10 minutes (see Basics)*
Baby yellow squash, *sliced in half lengthwise*
Japanese eggplant, *sliced in half lengthwise*
Sweet bell peppers, *whole or cut in half or quarters*
Hot peppers, *whole*
Asparagus spears, *whole*
Tomatoes, *whole (use small ones)*
Green onions, *whole*
Fennel, *1/4" horizontal slices of the bulb*
Mushrooms, *whole or cut, according to size*
Zucchini, *sliced in half lengthwise*
Garlic (see Grilled Whole Garlic)
Etc...

Basted with
1/4 cup olive oil
1 tbsp. tamari (preferable) or soy sauce
1 tbsp. oriental toasted sesame oil (optional)

1) In a bowl or cup, mix olive oil and tamari or soy sauce.
2) For all vegetables, except corn, place on grill and baste frequently with oil mixture (use a basting brush if available). Turn and cook until browned to taste. (Approx. 5 minutes).
3) When grilling vegetables such as the potatoes, squash, and eggplant, add sesame oil to the olive oil mixture.
4) Corn can be cooked by simply placing it in its husk on the grill directly over hot coals and rotating it every couple of minutes for approximately 12 minutes. (Don't get nervous when the outside husk chars.) This method of cooking tends to slightly caramelize the kernels, giving the corn a sweeter flavor than if it were boiled. To avoid the kernels browning slightly (which I find adds to the flavor), soak the corn in water, in its husk, for 20 minutes before grilling.
5) Serve on warmed plates.

LE SECRET: Serve directly from the grill. Grilled vegetables go limp very quickly. The best grill flavor comes from real hardwood charcoal.
ADVENTURE CLUB: Place any combination on a wooden skewer and make vegetable shish keBobs.
GARNISH: Lemon or orange twist.
SUGGESTED ACCOMPANIMENTS: Herbed butter (see Building a Better Butter). As a meal, serve with any kind of rice.
MUSIC TO GRILL BY: k.d. lang, *Shadowland*.
WINE: Pinot Noir [red].

One Potato, Two Potato

Tin Foil Potatoes

(SERVES TWO)

A quick added bonus for any BBQ'd meal.

INGREDIENTS

8 new potatoes or 2 regular potatoes (exact number may vary with size), *skin on, sliced 1/4" thick*
Fresh herbs: 3 large sprigs of rosemary, thyme, and/or dill, *stems removed*
Onions: 1 medium onion or 4 scallions or 16 chives or 1 leek, *sliced 1/4" thick*
Fresh ground black pepper and salt, to taste
6 tbsp. olive oil (flavored if available)
2 cloves of garlic, *minced or finely sliced*
3 feet of tin foil

1) Place sliced potatoes on tin foil, no more than two slices deep.
2) Add any or all of the suggested ingredients on top.
3) Sprinkle with olive oil.
4) Fold tin foil so that it is sealed.
5) Place over hot BBQ coals for 25 minutes (grilling time may vary according to size and flame). Turn frequently. Two thirds of the way through grilling, poke a couple of fork holes in the tin foil to allow the charcoal flavor to permeate. (Be careful, escaping oil may cause flames to flare up.)

ALTERNATIVES: May be baked in an oven for 45 minutes at 350 degrees.

Sesame Yams

(SERVES TWO)

Convincing evidence for why I consider yams to be one of the most underrated vegetables. Serve with any meal, or add a couple Chinese greens (i.e., Bok Choy), and a sliced yellow Italian squash — and call it dinner.

2 medium sized yams, *skin on, sliced 1/4" thick*
2 tbsp. toasted Oriental sesame oil
2 tbsp. butter
1 leek, or 6 scallions, *sliced crosswise 1/4" thick and washed thoroughly*
1 - 3 cloves of garlic, *minced*
2 - 4 inches of fresh ginger root, *peeled and grated*
Fresh ground black pepper, to taste

1) Steam yams for 10 minutes (see Basics).
2) In a sauté pan over med-high heat, melt butter and sauté your choice of green onions for 3 - 5 minutes or until browned.
3) Add sesame oil, yams, and all other ingredients. Sauté until yams have reached desired degree of crispness. (I sauté for up to 20 minutes to really brown the lot.)

ALTERNATIVES: Sweet potatoes may be substituted for yams.
NOTES: The dinner version cooks nicely in a wok.

FLAVORED OLIVE OIL

(MAKES 1 LITER BOTTLE)
A great all purpose pick-me-up for bread (especially bruschetta), pasta, pizza, avocados, tomatoes, etc.

INGREDIENTS
1 liter (or quart) bottle of olive oil (works equally well with plain and virgin varieties)
4 garlic cloves, *peeled and cut in half*
2 tsp. whole black, white, or mixed color peppercorns
4 whole dried hot peppers
1 large fresh sprig of rosemary, *stem on*
1 large fresh sprig of thyme, *stem on*

1) Soak label off bottle and remove plastic pouring spout.
2) Pour out top 1/2" of oil to make room for ingredients.
3) Add ingredients to oil.
4) Replace plastic pouring spout (now conveniently doubling as a strainer), cover with screw cap, and leave
   for at least 2 days.

LE SECRET: To maximize the visual aesthetic, choose the longest rosemary and thyme stems available.
Place herbs in bottle with the base of the stem at the bottom. Use a chopstick or fondue fork to create an
appealing arrangement.
ADVENTURE CLUB: Create your own personalized labels and bring oil to a dinner in place of wine.
For added visual appeal, use clear, fancy-shaped bottles capped with a wine cork or Grolsh beer bottles that
come with a permanantly attached top.
ALTERNATIVES: Spiced vinegars can be made in a similar manner using the more delicate flavoring
agents such as thyme.
NOTES: (i) Make sure that oil covers all contents to prevent mold from forming. (ii) The International Olive
Oil Council's manual states that flavored oils should be refrigerated and consumed in 2 days. Let this fact
be your guide. Although I am not encouraging you to follow my irreverent ways (in this particular instance),
I keep my flavored oil for up to one month and display it on my kitchen counter.
MUSIC TO FLAVOR BY: Bob Dylan, *Highway 61 Revisited.*

REHYDRATION OF SUN-DRIED TOMATOES

(MAKES TWO CUPS)

A home-made alternative to the expensive gourmet store variety. Sun-dried tomatoes in oil can be served as is, with antipasto, or used as an ingredient.

INGREDIENTS

3 oz. package of dried sun-dried tomatoes
1 cup virgin olive oil
2 tsp. honey
2 tsp. balsamic vinegar
1 mason jar, approximately 12 ounces

Your choice of:
2 fresh rosemary sprigs, *stem on*
2 fresh thyme sprigs, *stem on*
3 garlic cloves, *peeled and cut in half*

1) Place dried tomatoes in a colander or strainer and rinse them with hot tap water for 4 minutes.
2) Drain all water and place tomatoes in an empty mason jar. Layer with a selection of the flavor-enhancing herbs.
3) In a separate cup, mix the honey and vinegar with the oil. Pour mixture over tomatoes until all of the contents are covered. (Add extra oil if required.)
4) Store jar in a cool dry place for 3 days.

LE SECRET: Rinse the tomatoes thoroughly. This process "unseals" the tomatoes and allows them to absorb the oil.
ADVENTURE CLUB: After consuming the tomatoes, use the remaining oil for bruschetta, salads, or pasta.
NOTES: If the contents are not all covered in oil, mold may form.
MUSIC TO SUN BY: Elvis Presley, *The Sun Sessions*.

54

BUILDING A BETTER BUTTER

Herbed and flavored butters are a snap to prepare and add extra savor and a sophisticated touch to any meal. Serve with bread, or use as an instant glaze for meats, fish, poultry, rice, and vegetables.

SUGGESTED COMBINATIONS:

Herb butter: 4 tbsp. of any of the following fresh herbs: basil, dill, tarragon, thyme, oregano, mint, or any combination thereof, *stems removed, chopped finely* + 2 tbsp. lemon juice.

Sante Fe butter: 1/2 tsp. crushed chili peppers, 1 1/2 tbsp. lime juice + 3 tbsp. fresh cilantro, *chopped finely.*

Chive butter: 4 tbsp. chives, *chopped finely.*

Garlic butter: 1 garlic clove, *minced* + 2 tbsp. of any fresh herb listed above.

Pernod butter: 1 tbsp. Pernod (an alcohol) + 2 tbsp. fennel tops, *chopped finely.*

Grand Marnier butter: 1 tbsp. Grand Marnier or Cointreau (alcohols) + zest of 1/2 orange.

Combine with
1/4 lb. stick of butter (salted or unsalted, according to taste)
6 inches of tin foil.

1) Soften butter by leaving it at room temperature for 1 hour. In a bowl mash butter with a fork and add ingredients. Blend thoroughly and then either:
   Place on tin foil or wax paper and roll into a butter log approximately 1 1/4" in diameter; or
   Press into any small mold or cookie cutter.
2) Return to refrigerator until butter hardens. To serve the log version, remove tin foil and slice into 1/4" ovals.
   For the molded version, remove from refrigerator, let stand for 3 minutes and then tap out of mold onto serving plate.

ADVENTURE CLUB: Experiment with your own combination of ingredients.
GARNISH: Garnish butter plate with a sprig, dash, or twist of one of the ingredients.
ALTERNATIVES: Butter can be replaced with margarine. Fresh ground black pepper, to taste, may be added to any of the butters.
NOTES: Herbed butter may be frozen.
MUSIC TO CHURN BY: Glen Gould, *Bach, The Goldberg Variations.*

10 WAYS TO AVOID MAKING DESSERT

Let them eat cake.

— Marie Antoinette

1) When your dinner guest calls in the afternoon to politely ask if he/she can bring anything, ask him/her to swing by a fine bakery for a few harmlessly sinful pastries (1 per guest).
2) Serve premium ice cream, frozen yogurt, sherbert, or gelato, either directly from the container or topped with:
   - fresh strawberries, raspberries, blueberries, mangoes, kiwis, etc.
   - bananas kissed with brown sugar*
   - an atrociously rich brownie
   - M&M's
   - A crumbled Heath chocolate bar
3) Flambé** any of the preceeding ice cream combinations with a tablespoon of one of the following: Grand Marnier, Cointreau, Sambuca, Framboise, Dark Rum, etc.
4) Top vanilla or chocolate ice cream with crème de menthe liqueur and serve with chocolates, or shower with chocolate flakes using a regular grater to grate any solid chunk of white or dark chocolate.
5) After a light meal, serve a selection of very ripe cheeses.
6) After a heavy meal, serve a selection of fresh (and, if possible, exotic) fruits.
7) After a BBQ, bring out a bag of marshmallows and watch your "grown-up" friends regress to childhood before your eyes.
8) Serve freshly brewed, flavored coffee. Or spike freshly brewed coffee with your favorite liqueur and top with whipped cream (optional).
9) Serve a dessert wine or port.
10) Have sex instead.

* This one bends the rules a bit. In a sauté pan over med-high heat, melt 2 tbsp. of butter and add 3 tsp. brown sugar. After sugar melts, add one or more sliced bananas and sauté for 3 minutes. Pour contents over vanilla, chocolate, or coffee ice cream. For Adventure Club members, before removing bananas from sauté pan, add an ounce of dark rum or hazelnut or coffee liqueur and touch a flame to the liquid. (Be sure to follow flambé precautions.)

** To flambé, place alcohol in a tablespoon. Using a match, lighter or candle, heat underside of spoon for 10 seconds and then touch flame directly to liquid. While liquid is burning, pour over ice cream. For added melodrama, dim lights and pour from 1 foot above plate. Do not do this near anything flammable (i.e., tablecloths or napkins).

BANANA FRENCH TOAST

(SERVES TWO)
Sinfully delicious. Ideal for Sunday mornings.

INGREDIENTS
4 eggs
1/3 cup milk (any kind will do)
1 1/2 tsp. ground cinnamon (no sugar) or nutmeg (but not both)
4 slices of whole wheat bread, multi-grain bread, or nut bread, *sliced to the same thickness as conventional white bread*
2 ripe bananas, *1 peeled and sliced into 1/4" slices, the second, skin on for use as a garnish*
1 tbsp. butter
1/2 cup real maple syrup

1) Beat eggs, milk, and half of the cinnamon *or* nutmeg in a shallow bowl.
2) Soak bread slices in egg mixture until completely soggy.
3) Take one slice of bread, cover with banana slices, and then cover with a second slice of bread (like a drippy banana sandwich).
4) In a sauté pan, over med-high heat, melt butter. Add "sandwich." Cover pan with lid. Cook until well browned on both sides and cooked throughout (approximately 4 minutes on the first side and 3 minutes on the second side).
5) Remove "sandwich" from pan and place on warmed serving plates. Remove pan from burner and quickly pour maple syrup into hot pan for 15 seconds.
6) Pour syrup over "sandwich."

LE SECRET: The object is to brown the outside nicely and cook the inside thoroughly without drying it out. Make an incision in the middle to test for doneness. If the outside is done but the inside is still runny, reduce heat to medium-low and cover for a couple more minutes.
ADVENTURE CLUB: Sex after breakfast. If sex is out of the question, try replacing bananas with slices of fresh peaches, apricots, or other fruits.
GARNISH: Three 1/4" slices of banana, in its skin, side by side, and remaining cinnamon or nutmeg sprinkled around the edge of the plate.
SUGGESTED ACCOMPANIMENTS: Any type of fresh berries.
ALTERNATIVES: In a pinch, even Wonder bread will do. Avoid pumpernickel and other heavy breads. Maple syrup may be substituted with any other type of syrup.
NOTES: It is o.k. for syrup to bubble slightly in pan.
MUSIC TO COOK BY: Chet Baker, *Let's Get Lost* (Soundtrack).
WINE: Champagne and fresh squeezed orange juice (1 part champagne, 2 parts orange juice).

weekend omelets

(SERVES TWO)

Omelets are a variation on the theme of pizzas. The eggs, like the pizza dough, provide a blank canvas on which to create. The only obstacle between you and a delicious omelet, on a well deserved quiet weekend morning, is a little inspiration. Combine your favorite ingredients from the following groupings and paint your own picture.

INGREDIENTS

Fresh herbs

Basil, rosemary, thyme, oregano, tarragon, dill, mint, cilantro, Italian parsley...*stems removed*

Vegetables

Asparagus, spinach, tomatoes, radicchio, avocado, mushrooms, sweet peppers, green onions...*sliced into small pieces*

Accents

Garlic, *minced,* leeks, *sliced crosswise and washed thoroughly,* scallions, *sliced,* hot peppers, *diced finely*

Cheeses

Brie, Camembert, blue cheese, Swiss, Gruyère, aged Vermont cheddar, or any other flavorful cheese, *cut into 1/4"
cubes, grated, or crumbled*

Meats

Bacon, *cooked and chopped,* prosciutto, cooked ham, smoked salmon, *all sliced*

Combine with

4 eggs

2 tbsp. butter

Salt and pepper, to taste

1) In a frying pan, cook meats (if not already cooked or cured) and drain off fat. Reserve.
2) In a sauté pan, over med-high heat, melt 1 tbsp. butter. Sauté accents for 2 minutes, add denser vegetables, sauté for 2 more minutes, and then add remaining vegetables, cooked meats, and herbs for 2 more minutes. Remove contents from pan and reserve in a warmed bowl.
3) Place eggs in a bowl and beat with a fork or whisk.
4) Over medium heat use the same sauté pan to melt 1 tbsp. butter. Add beaten eggs and immediately sprinkle cheese over eggs. Cover for 2 minutes.
5) Sprinkle reserved ingredients over partially cooked egg mixture and cook until eggs are almost at the desired degree of firmness. Fold over with a spatula and heat until completely cooked.
6) Serve on a warmed plate.

LE SECRET: The more ingredients, especially fresh herbs, the merrier.
ADVENTURE CLUB: Top a subtly flavored omelet with black caviar.
GARNISH: A sprig of one of the herbs and/or an orange twist.
SUGGESTED ACCOMPANIMENTS: Muffins, fresh fruit, or hashbrown potatoes.
ALTERNATIVES: Go out for breakfast.
MUSIC TO COOK BY: Academy of St. Martin-in-the-Fields, *Bach, The Brandenburg Concertos.*
WINE: Fresh-brewed coffee.

One day a traveling businessman was driving down a country road. In the distance, he noticed a farmer standing in his field under an apple tree, surrounded by pigs. The farmer was systematically hoisting pig after pig up to the branches so they could eat their fill of apples. When each pig had eaten its fill, he would put it down and pick up another. This mystified the time-conscious businessman. When he was within earshot, he stopped his car and shouted, "Hey Mister, you could save a lot of time if you just shook the tree and let 'em eat the apples off the ground." The farmer looked up and in his slow-but-wise country drawl replied, "What's time to a pig?"

COCKTAILS

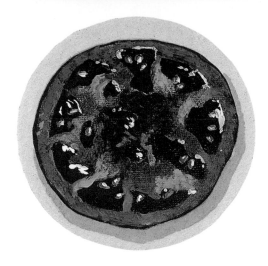

BLOODY MARYS

(SERVES ONE OR MORE)

Chances are, your senses have been dulled, if not totally obliterated, by the pre-fab
Bloody Mary mixes used by most bars. In this recipe, "T" stands for taste.

INGREDIENTS	FULL PITCHER	ONE GLASS
Real tomato juice (canned but not reconstituted)	24 oz. can	6 oz.
Lemon juice	Juice of 1 lemon	1 tsp. lemon juice
Worcestershire sauce	1 1/2 tsp.	3 shakes
Tabasco sauce	1/2 tsp.	2 shakes
Salt	1/3 tsp.	2 shakes
Pepper	1/3 tsp.	2 shakes or turns
Horseradish (Optional)	1/2 tsp.	1/8 tsp.
Vodka	6 oz.	1 1/2 oz.
Ice		

LE SECRET: Spice to order. Ask your guest what their spice threshold is on a scale of 1 - 10,
and spice accordingly.
ADVENTURE CLUB: Use a pepper vodka (Absolut and Stoli make good ones).
GARNISH: Salted rim,* celery stalk (leafy top half, if possible), and lemon wedge.
ALTERNATIVES: Replace tomato juice with Clamato juice (known as a Bloody Caesar) or V8 juice.
STIRRING MUSIC: Bernard Herrmann, *Vertigo* (Alfred Hitchcock's movie soundtrack).

* To salt the rim:
1) Place a thin layer of celery salt or salt in a small dish or bowl.
2) Take empty glass and moisten its rim with a lemon wedge.
3) Dip rim in salt. Shake off excess.

MARGARITAS

(SERVES ONE)

This recipe is based on a *Los Angeles Times* story about a 90-year-old Tijuana pioneer named Danny Herrera, who, as the story was reported, invented the margarita in 1947 to impress a beautiful brunette showgirl and sometimes-actress named Majorie (Margarita in Spanish). His original recipe is as follows:

INGREDIENTS
1 1/2 oz. white tequila
1 oz. Cointreau
1/2 oz. lemon juice, *freshly squeezed* (1 lemon)
1/2 cup shaved (or crushed) ice

1) Salt rim of glass.*
2) Place all ingredients in a shaker and shake.
3) Strain or serve with ice.

To make frozen margaritas, add 1 1/2 cups crushed ice and blend in a blender until liquid resembles a slush drink.

LE SECRET: Don't tell Danny, but the secret is to replace white tequila with gold tequila.
ADVENTURE CLUB: Replace Cointreau with Grand Marnier.
GARNISH: A wheel or a wedge of lime.
ALTERNATIVES: Triple Sec may be used in place of Cointreau. Freshly squeezed limes or Rose's Lime Juice may be used in place of lemon juice.
MUSIC TO HAT DANCE BY: Flaco Jimenze, *Ay Te Dejo en San Antonio*.

* To salt the rim:
1) Place a thin layer of salt in a small dish or bowl.
2) Take empty glass and moisten its rim with a lemon wedge.
3) Dip rim in salt.

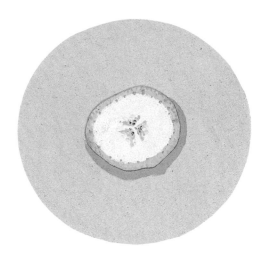

FROZEN FRUIT DAIQUIRIES

(A BLENDER FULL)
Hot fun in the summertime.

INGREDIENTS
5 oz. amber or dark rum
Juice of 2 lemons
Juice of 2 limes
2 tbsp. sugar (brown sugar if possible)
3 bananas, *peeled,* or 2 cups of strawberries, *tops removed* (or any combination thereof)
2 cups crushed ice
Place all ingredients in a blender, ice last, and blend.

LE SECRET: Use very ripe fruit to take full advantage of its natural sugar content.
ADVENTURE CLUB: Try mangoes, peaches, or more exotic fruits.
GARNISH: Place a slice of the fruit on the lip of the glass. For bananas, cut a 1/4" slice of banana with its skin on, make one cut outward from the center and slide onto the rim of the glass.
ALTERNATIVES: In the off-season, substitute fresh fruit with frozen raspberries or strawberries.
NOTES: Daiquiries are intended to be tart. If the drink is too tart for your taste, use riper fruit, add more sugar, or use frozen fruit packaged in a sugar syrup.
MUSIC TO BLEND BY: Manteca, *Perfect Foot.*

VODKA & FRESH SQUEEZED ORANGE JUICE

(SERVES ONE)

To the uninitiated, the distinction between freshly squeezed orange juice and any other form of the juice, may seem insignificant. Trust me, freshly squeezed juice makes a run-of-the-mill screwdriver an otherworldly concoction.*

INGREDIENTS
6 oz. fresh squeezed orange juice, *squeezed just before serving*
1 1/4 oz. vodka, *chilled, if possible*
1 wedge of lemon or lime
4 ice cubes

1) Pour ingredients into a glass, stir, and go directly to citrus heaven.

LE SECRET: It's all in the oranges.
ADVENTURE CLUB: Take the oranges from the bottom of the orange pyramid in your grocery store.
GARNISH: Lemon or lime wedge.
ALTERNATIVES: Fresh squeezed grapefruit juice.
NOTES: The best juice oranges are Valencia oranges. If they are unavailable, ask your produce manager for the sweetest, full-bodied juice orange (Beware! Many so-called "juice" oranges are given the name because they produce a lot of juice, but it is often thin and watery. "Eating" oranges such as Navel oranges are also less desirable because they produce very little juice.)
MUSIC TO SQUEEZE BY: Astor Piazzolla, *Tango: Zero Hour.*

* Exhaustive research recently conducted among 15 non-believers in a scientifically controlled environment (albeit at a poolside wedding reception, beside an orange grove, near Valencia, Spain) proved conclusively that my thesis is valid.

MARTINIS

(SERVES ONE)

There are as many combinations and permutations of martini recipes and serving styles as there are bartenders in white shirts and funny little bow ties who make them. I will begin with a "standard" recipe and follow it with a glossary of options.

INGREDIENTS

2 - 3 oz. gin
1/2 oz. dry vermouth
Martini shaker and strainer (In a pinch, use an oversized glass and strain manually)

1) Fill shaker with ice.
2) Add gin.
3) Add 1/2 oz. of vermouth.
4) Stir for 15 seconds.
5) Strain into a pre-chilled martini glass.
6) Garnish with an olive.

GLOSSARY OF TERMS AND OPTIONS

VARIATIONS
Gin Martini Made with gin (the standard).
Vodka Martini Made with vodka.
007 Made with 2 parts vodka, one part gin (James Bond's favorite...shaken, not stirred, of course).

VERMOUTH GUIDELINES
Regular Martini 1/4 - 1/2 ounce of vermouth.
Dry Martini Pour 1/2 ounce of vermouth into shaker. Swirl it around and then pour it out. (The object of this is to coat the wall of the shaker.) Fill shaker with ice, add gin or vodka. Stir and strain.
Extra-Dry Martini (Follow these directions for anybody who pauses before enunciating the word "extra.") Fill shaker with ice and add gin or vodka. Pick up vermouth bottle and wave it past the top of the shaker. Stir and strain.

GARNISHES
Olive One or two green olives stuffed with pimentos.
Twist A tiny strip of a lemon rind cut from the yellow outer layer of the lemon peel. Its name is derived from the fact that it is twisted to release its natural oils. Run the twisted strip along the rim of the martini glass, coating the rim with a fine layer of tart oil, and then drop it into the glass.
Onion The use of small cocktail onions as a garnish transforms the drink into a "Gibson."

SERVING METHODS
On the rocks Over ice.
Straight up No ice (although the martini is always mixed over ice first and then strained).

MIXING METHODS
Shaken Place cap on shaker and shake six times.
Stirred In order to avoid "bruising" the gin or vodka the drink is stirred.

LE SECRET: The three crucial questions to ask when making anybody a martini:
1) Olive or twist (or "Oliver Twist?"). 2) Straight up or on the rocks? 3) Regular, dry, or extra dry?
ADVENTURE CLUB: Live like James Bond for a day.
GARNISH: See garnish options above.
MUSIC TO SHAKE BY: Frank Sinatra, *Songs for Swingin' Lovers.*

THE ART OF:

THE ART OF PRESENTATION

The first taste is with the eyes.
—Attributed to Sophocles

Part of the pleasure of cooking for company is basking in the "oohs and aahs" that welcome a carefully presented plate as it is placed on the table. Painting with food comes naturally to some people. Others are somewhat oblivious to the concept. I tend to fret over presentation even when eating alone. For the uninitiated, here's a quick roadmap to presentation.

CONCEPTUALIZATION: After deciding what to serve, pause for a moment and let your mind's eye focus on the plate. Think about the colors of the main food element as well as the vegetables, rice, etc. that will accompany it. Avoid mixing foods that are all the same color (i.e. several green vegetables). Think about how you might position the food on the plate. Then ask yourself, will this be visually pleasing? If the answer is no, think about using a different plate or garnish, or consider substituting a vegetable that will add color and pizzazz. God's gift to the art of presentation is the full color spectrum in which He/She created vegetables. When shopping, look for brightly colored bell peppers, carrots, squash, string beans, etc. to accent other colors on the plate.

Before preparing the food, think of how each element will "sit" in relation to the others. For example, when serving carrots, will they look best sliced lengthwise, widthwise, or on an angle? Or should you cook them whole with a bit of the green top left intact (nouvelle carrot style)?

EXECUTION: Instead of dishing out the meal's components haphazardly, take a moment to artfully arrange them on the plate. Simple symmetric lines and circular patterns are the easiest to create and usually the most visually rewarding. Use color, texture, size, and shape to balance the grouping. It's often easier to create a pattern by first designating how the plate will sit in front of the diner. This is especially useful when creating a fan-like pattern.

Check to see that all of the food is at its radiant best. A quick glaze of lemon or butter can add sparkle to vegetables. For some foods, such as pastas or salads, you can "cheat" the presentation by bringing the more colorful or delectable ingredients to the top.

Just before serving, wipe any sauce or drippings from the edge of the plate.

GARNISHING: Twenty years ago a garnish was a piece of parsley. A fancy garnish was a piece of watercress. Today, French and Californian cooking styles have made garnishing an art. Don't be intimidated! Even Picasso had to start somewhere.
1) Choose colors that act as foils, accentuating the other colors on the plate.
2) Select garnishes that hint at the flavors in the meal (e.g. using basil leaves as a garnish for a pesto dish or fennel tops for a Pernod-flavored dish).
3) Add contrasting or exotic elements such as colorful fruits (cross sections of kiwis, star fruit, blood oranges, or papayas) or edible flowers.
4) Take advantage of the wide borders of oversized plates by framing the meal with a dusting of herbs or spices such as ground pepper, paprika, and/or finely chopped chives. Avoid "flavor leakage" by selecting from the existing pool of flavors and ingredients found in the dish.
5) Use chives to create patchwork patterns or to "bundle up" string beans or other thinly sliced vegetables.

STEAL FROM THE BEST: Take note of the presentation tricks used by chefs in the restaurants you patronize or magazines you read. Many presentation techniques explain themselves and are easily duplicated.

PREVIEWING THE MEAL: For Adventure Club members and cooking eccentrics only. Upon walking in the door, dinner guests generally head for either the bar or the kitchen. In situations where you are preparing the food with your guests present, heighten their anticipation by taking a minute before they arrive to artfully arrange the raw ingredients (known in France as mise en place) on your kitchen counter.

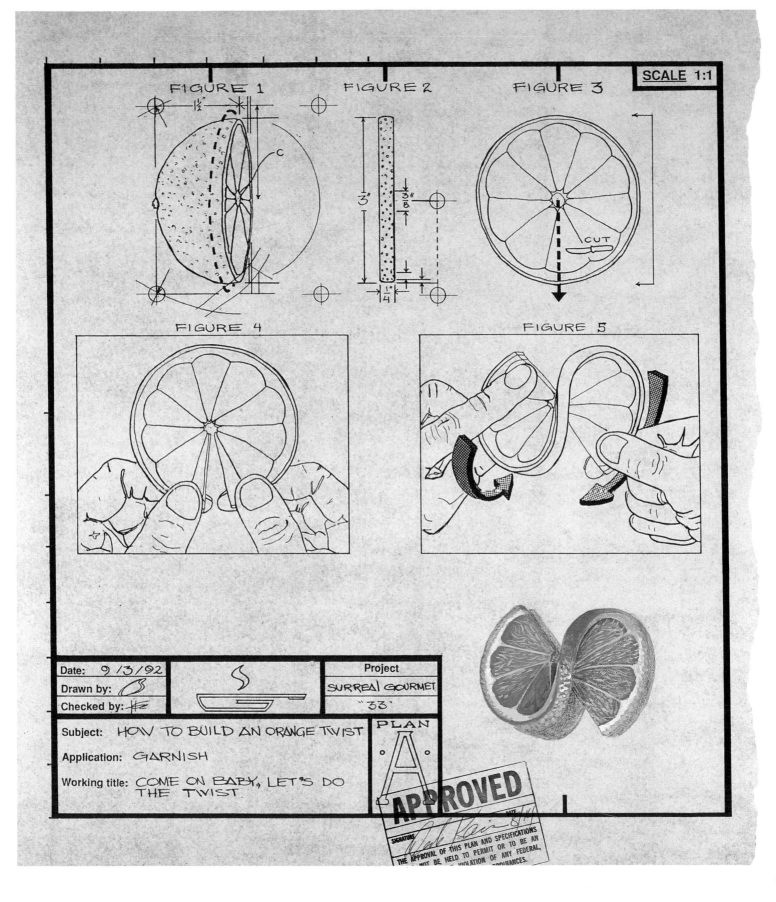

FIGURE 1   FIGURE 2   FIGURE 3

SCALE 1:1

FIGURE 4

FIGURE 5

Date:	9/3/92			Project
Drawn by:				SURREAL GOURMET
Checked by:				"33"

Subject: HOW TO BUILD AN ORANGE TWIST

Application: GARNISH

Working title: COME ON BABY, LET'S DO THE TWIST.

PLAN A

APPROVED

THE ART OF SAUTÉING

Simply stated, sautéing is a sophisticated version of pan cooking meets wok cooking. The sauté method provides speed, control, and versatility. Once you get comfortable with the sautéing method, you will be able to prepare fast, fresh, tasty meals with less fuss and mess. For example, a whole boneless chicken breast will sauté in less than a fourth of the time it would take to bake on the bone.

THE HEAT SOURCE: Unfortunately, most people have no control over a key part of the process. Sautéing is faster, easier, and more exact over a gas stove. There is but one solution for those with electric elements. Move.

THE PAN: Sauté pans come in many sizes, but one standard shape. The rounded sides are designed to allow the turning of food with a flick of the wrist, by tossing it off the back side of the pan (see illustration). Professional pans have teflon-like coatings that prevent sticking and help brown food evenly. Never touch these coatings with anything but plastic cooking utensils. Very serious chefs use non-coated blue steel (also known as French steel) pans. To avoid sticking, they use well greased pans and keep the food moving.

BUTTER/OIL/MARGARINE: Butter, oil, and margarine all work well in the sauté pan, although margarine is the least desirable of the three. A good non-stick pan will reduce the amount of fat required. In order to keep butter from burning and browning, fastidious chefs clarify their butter (see Basics). Use only vegetable oils. Most other types tend to burn.

SAUTE TECHNIQUE: To master the technique of sauteing, begin by taking a moment to think about how the ingredients will cook, consider their consistency and the flavors you are blending. The trick is to ensure that every one of the ingredients cooks to its own degree of perfection and that the flavors blend as desired.

1) Ingredients that will take longer to cook should be cut into smaller pieces.
2) Pat dry meats, fish, and chicken with a paper towel or clean cloth to remove excess moisture.
3) It is important to wait until the butter or oil in the pan is extremely hot before adding the ingredients. The hot pan sears the food, sealing in the flavors and moisture. As a result, the food absorbs less of the oil or butter.
4) Start by sautéing the flavoring ingredients such as garlic, ginger, onions, or peppers for approximately two minutes until lightly brown. This "unlocks" their flavor and allows them to "marry" with the other ingredients. The finer the chop, the more the flavor will blend.
5) Sauté foods in declining order of density starting with the densest. When using extremely dense vegetables, such as potatoes, steam them for 5 -10 minutes first (see Basics).
6) You've seen professional chefs do it. It's all in the wrist action. Most foods will cook thoroughly and evenly over high heat if constantly turned (see illustration). The hotter the heat and the more frequently the ingredients are tossed, the more flavor will be sealed in. (The exception is flat pieces of meat which are usually turned only once.) Practice flipping eggs over-easy in the privacy of your own kitchen. If you tend towards exuberance, practice with an apron.
7) For meats such as chicken or pork that must be fully cooked, sear the outside first on high heat and then cover pan, reduce the heat and finish cooking.

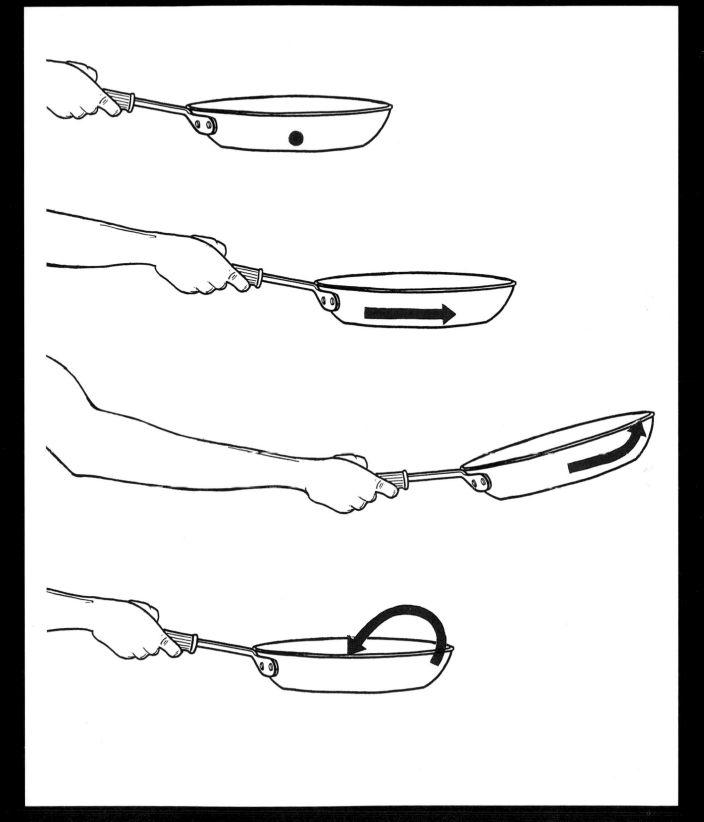

THE ART OF THE SALAD
(AN APPENDIX TO THE CAESAR SALAD RECIPE)

Scott Wilson is a college buddy of mine who earned his way through school waiting tables in a restaurant that specialized in Caesar salads prepared tableside. In 1980, Scott gave me my first Caesar salad lesson over the telephone, after I'd woken him at 2 o'clock in the afternoon (ah – college life!). Since then, I have made literally hundreds of Caesars at home and in friends' kitchens around the world. Between mouthfuls of salad and sips of wine, relationships have begun and ended, business deals have succeeded and failed, and New Year's Eves have come and gone. Contrary to what anyone in a white hat might tell you, there are no secret ingredients or professional tricks. Subtle variations of ingredients and the manner in which they are assembled will make or break a Caesar salad. To help in your quest for the quintessential Caesar, I have attempted to isolate the most essential, difficult, and fickle components.

THE BOWL: Some people and most restaurants commit a sacrilegious mistake right off the bat by eschewing the bowl, opting instead for a blender or food processor to mix the dressing. This method whips the yolk, giving the dressing an undesirable mayonnaise-like texture. The definitive salad begins with a large unfinished wooden bowl (i.e. not coated with a shiny lacquer). The rough interior wall of the bowl provides a perfect surface for blending the ingredients. The best bowls are usually bored out of one solid slab of tree. When asked to make my salad for a party – an event that has become my 15 minutes of reoccuring fame – I always bring my own bowl. Pool sharks travel with their own cues; the concept is the same.

THE BLENDING METHOD: Once the aforementioned bowl is in hand, facilitating the successful marriage of the ingredients becomes an intensely physical activity. Using the back side of a soup spoon and a healthy amount of pressure, grind the ingredients one at a time in a repetitive circular motion against the entire interior wall of the bowl. It will take approximately 15 seconds (the garlic and anchovies will take longer) for each new ingredient to blend with the existing ingredients and form a smooth paste.

THE CHEESE: This is probably the single most important ingredient of the perfect Caesar. Italian Parmigiano-Reggiano is produced exclusively in a small region of northern-central Italy. Its distinctive taste and grainy texture are unmistakable. Cheese makers from this region adhere to a stringent code of rules regarding what the cows are fed and how long the cheese is aged (at least 2 years). A food writer at *The Los Angeles Times* wrote, "Once you get a taste of the real stuff — crumbly, earthy and rich as wine — there's no turning back: Everything else is sawdust." The disparity is most easily likened to the difference between champagne produced by the traditional méthode champenoise in the French province of Champagne and all other sparkling wines. (Sparkling wine lovers should disregard this analogy.) After you have added Parmigiano-Reggiano to your cooking repertoire, you will be forced to adopt guerilla defense tactics to protect the ungrated cheese. Roaming dinner guests tend to circle the wedge like hungry sharks, and will devour it the second you turn to spin-dry the lettuce.

THE GARLIC: Use only fresh garlic. Anything less than direct-from-the-bulb is a sacrifice of disastrous magnitude. (See Staple Spices for more about garlic selection.) Medical researchers in Gilroy, California, the self-proclaimed garlic capital of the world, recently perfected *The Instant Garlic Diet* ®. Dieters do not in fact lose weight, but they look much thinner from a distance.

THE LETTUCE: Romaine is the Godfather of Caesar lettuces because it "wears" the heavy dressing so well. If you must substitute, use another hearty lettuce. After washing the lettuce, use a lettuce spinner or a towel to remove all water. Water from wet leaves dilutes the dressing. For maximum crispness, return the prepared lettuce to the refrigerator until just before serving. If you are preparing the lettuce hours in advance, you can avoid browning edges by cutting the leaves with a sharp knife instead of tearing them.

THE ANCHOVY: Don't be intimidated. Like most people, I hate the sight and taste of anchovies. However, when blended along with the other ingredients into a paste, the distinctive anchovy taste is unidentifiable. Then why use it? Because along with the garlic and Dijon mustard, the anchovy provides the essence of the Caesar flavor, which all the remaining ingredients serve to enhance. Modern technology has graced us with fish in a tube. Anchovy paste blends well and provides the perfect solution to the old problem of using one anchovy and having the rest of the school spoil before the next salad.

THE CROUTONS: Nothing is more anticlimactic then topping a finely tuned Caesar with store-bought croutons intended for turkey stuffing. Homemade croutons, fashioned from any leftover thickly sliced bread, are the hidden jewels of the salad. (See Basics for a simple crouton recipe.) "Gourmet-style" croutons made by cottage industry suppliers are a suitable replacement for making your own. My only complaint is the exorbitant price they command for what is essentially seasoned stale bread.

THE LEGACY: A great Caesar should knock you off your chair, then hit you again as you struggle to regain your senses. I can appreciate the fact that not everyone likes to wrestle with their salad in this manner, but that's why man created Thousand Island dressing. If you elect to leave out the garlic or use the ingredients sparingly, please don't tell anyone that the recipe came from this book.

(A well-worn garlic bowl will register
1/2 clove even when empty.)

When I think of dishwashing, I think of the children's story about a bachelor who never washed his dishes. Finally, when there was nothing left to eat from, he loaded all of the dishes onto a flatbed truck and drove them through a rainstorm. The notion of looking forward to doing the dishes is foreign to me. The possibility would never have entered my mind if it hadn't been for a discussion about this book with singer-songwriter Corey Hart.

Corey passionately described how dishwashing can be rewarding — perhaps even as much as cooking. To my surprise, many of my friends nodded with understanding when I described this revelation. Researching the subject was less attractive to me than testing wines, so I asked Corey to contribute his thoughts.

ZEN AND THE ART OF DISHWASHING

BY COREY HART

I can easily remember back to a time when I believed dishes a dirty little affair I would have no part of. The task of making myself a decent toast and jam were challenge enough for my limited skills in the kitchen. Aah! but today, as maturity sets in, I come clean and confess to being a devout disciple of dishwashing. Ridicule me not. Epiphany can be experienced from behind the kitchen sink. Here are a few notes to remember when practicing the art of dishwashing.

1) Choose your cleaning brush with care, like you would a soul mate.

2) Perform the rites no later than 3 hours after the meal and witty conversations have ended.

3) Follow traditionalist values — "Mano a mano" (hand to hand). Wearing gloves is an absurd concept. You must feel the water and the dishes. Dishwashing machines are a cursed species. Of course, this goes against everything 20th century technology would have us believe. But consider this: the machine will never break or bruise a single item. You, on the other hand, are bonding…glasses may shatter, china will fall. So be it.

4) Don't rush the process. Relax. Daydream. Let the dishes communicate with you. Take each item individually and ask yourself existential questions. "Who am I?" "Why am I here?" "What is the true meaning of life?" "What time are the Montreal Canadians playing on T.V. tonight?" We are all individuals endowed with will and consciousness, finding ourselves in an alien world which possesses neither. We are for the most part self-creating beings. We are not initially given our complete character and goals, but must choose them by acts of pure decision. Dishes and their washing can be used as a conduit for these existential leaps. Contrast the existence of the natural object, e.g., a big silver fork, with the dramatics of your own human existence. Now that I've completely lost myself, I shall promptly go to the sink and interact with my spaghetti and meatball dishes.

MUSIC: Music is not necessary in this Zen pursuit. However if rhythm is desperately needed, try *I Can See Clearly Now* by Johnny Nash. Then continue with your sojourn.

NOTE: Your dishwashing soap should be environmentally friendly, 100% organic and biodegradable, containing no phosphates or perfumes. My favorite flavor is naturally scented lemon.

STAPLES:

STAPLE INGREDIENTS

A checklist of basic ingredients required for the preparation of the meals in this book.

OILS

Basic olive oil: Greek, Italian, or Spanish are preferred. The best buys are gallon cans* found in ethnic markets.

Virgin (or extra virgin or first cold pressing) olive oil: The wine of the '90s. A simple rule of thumb is to only use virgin (instead of basic) oil in situations where its nutty flavor can be easily distinguished (i.e., on delicately flavored pastas, on breads, in simple salad dressings, etc.). Before spending great sums of money, educate yourself by taste-testing several varieties on small squares of French bread. (Specialty food shops with in-house catering will often let you taste before you buy.)

Safflower or sunflower oil: Good all purpose cooking oils.

Oriental toasted sesame oil: More of a seasoning than an oil. A teaspoon is usually all that's needed to add flavor to wok cooking, grilling, marinades, etc.

Walnut oil: Great for delicate salads. Be sure to keep refrigerated.

VINEGARS

Red wine vinegar: Basic salad vinegar.

Flavored vinegars (herbed, raspberry, etc.): For marinating and flavored salad dressing.

Balsamic vinegar: A richer aged version of red wine vinegar.

SAUCES

Tamari sauce: A richer, aged version of soy sauce, made without wheat.

Soy sauce: The salt of the orient.

Worcestershire sauce: "From the recipe of a nobleman in the country," according to the label.

Tabasco sauce: Heating up Louisiana since 1868.

MISCELLANEOUS

Pesto: A traditional Italian sauce blended from fresh basil, garlic, parmesan cheese, olive oil, and pine nuts. A few years ago if you wanted pesto, you had to make it yourself. Now, excellent fresh pesto is available in most specialty food stores and in many supermarkets at a reasonable price. Spend your cooking time on something that will make more of a difference.

Sun-dried tomatoes: Available in specialty food shops, stored in oil. Most supermarkets now carry the infinitely less expensive dried version, which can be brought back to life by following the recipe for rehydration.

Pine nuts: One of the more flavorful survivors of the '80s food trends. Buy them in bulk. Keep refrigerated.

Pasta: Different shapes for different folks. Any form of pasta combined with the other staple ingredients on this list (and a small dose of imagination) will allow you to toss together a spontaneous pasta dish in about the same time it takes to prepare boxed macaroni and cheese.

Grated parmesan cheese: Use the less expensive pre-grated cheese for your cream sauces, pestos, and soups. If possible, buy freshly grated parmesan. In any case, avoid the type designed to have a long shelf life.

Imported Reggiano parmesan (ungrated): Use only where its distinctive flavor and texture can be appreciated (i.e., on salads and pastas). Always grate immediately prior to serving. For extra punch, use a coarser grate or wide shavings. (For more on the subject of risking one's life for this cheese, see The Art of the Salad.)

Dijon mustard: Starts where regular mustards leave off.

Most basic: Butter, cream, eggs, flour, onions, rice, lemons, limes, and oranges.

---

* The most innovative wine bucket I have ever seen in a restaurant was a beautifully decorated Greek olive oil can with the top removed by a can opener. (Be sure to flatten the sharp edges.)

STAPLE SPICES

**Once you have incorporated the following checklist of herbs and spices into
your daily cooking regimen, you need never cook a bland meal again.**

SALT & PEPPERS

Sea salt: Buy a large container and throw away your iodized salt. You won't notice any difference in flavor and your body will thank you.

Whole black peppercorns: A must. Use a grinder that can give you a coarse grind.

Whole multi-color peppercorns: Becoming quite popular, these colored peppercorns are hotter than ground black pepper and can add an interesting lift to your food. Do not use where the distinctive flavor of plain black pepper is an essential element of the dish (e.g., Caesar Salad or Steak au Poivre).

Ground cayenne pepper: A quick standby for spicing up certain dishes. Be careful. Cayenne pepper is so hot that the Los Angeles police use it in a chemical spray compound to subdue criminals.

REASONS TO LIVE

Fresh garlic: Accept no substitute! When buying garlic, look for a firm bulb. As it gets older and moves past its prime, the bulb loses its firmness and green sprouts appear in each clove.* Garlic is most pungent in its raw form. When it is baked or sautéed, it loses its big bite (so proportion accordingly). For those who like garlic, it can be used with most meat and vegetable dishes. At all costs, avoid dried, powdered garlic, the runt of the garlic family, and be wary of elephant garlic, a much blander version of the regular-sized bulb. Large garlic braids are decorative but impractical since they often dry out before you use all of the bulbs. Since the essence of this book is art, not science, I can't comment on claims that garlic has medicinal qualities. I will, however, share the observation that all my garlic-loving friends are exceptionally healthy human specimens.

Fresh ginger root: Fresh ginger can give or restore life to many meat and vegetable dishes. Grate finely when adding to marinades or soups. Use a coarser grate or slice for use in woks or when you want to give the taste buds (and sinuses) a real kick. Ginger root keeps for a couple weeks in the refrigerator and shrivels when old.

Fresh chili peppers: As a result of The Santa Fe Invasion, most markets carry a variety of fresh peppers ranging in strength from mild to suicidal. Ask your produce manager for assistance. Select them according to your taste buds and sweat glands. For those who enjoy the pain and pleasure principle of eating, a whole new world of stimulation awaits you. It's a good idea to experiment with small amounts before tossing in the whole pepper. Chop hot peppers finely and add them in the early stages of cooking. (Note: always wash your hands thoroughly immediately after cutting hot peppers. Otherwise the stimulation may not be where you want it to be!) Like garlic, chili peppers are strongest in their raw form, but they don't tame down as much when cooked. Eating very hot peppers raw is a very bad idea.

Dried whole chili peppers: Packaged dried whole chili peppers in varying degrees of intensity have become quite common. Chop them finely and add during cooking. Treat dried peppers with the same degree of respect required of fresh peppers. Hanging, dried pepper strands are the attractive-but-neglected offspring of the Southwestern cuisine craze. I frequently fantasize about forming a S.W.A.T. team of commando chefs whose mission it is to liberate unused strands from designer kitchens and deliver them to needy cooks. For those of you who promise to cook with your peppers, there are several companies in New Mexico, America's hot pepper heartland, that mail-order strands starting at $15. (See address in Basics.)

FRESH HERBS
(See The $100 Kitchen Revolution for herb garden inspiration)

Rosemary, Basil, Oregano, Thyme, Mint, Dill: Most markets now stock these herbs in their fresh produce departments. Fresh herbs have a totally different personality from the dried variety. Their flavors are much more immediate, especially in the raw form or when added in the final stages of cooking. When cooking with fresh herbs, especially for a long time, save some to add just before serving. This will "refresh" the flavor. Heat helps to draw the flavor out of dried herbs. To extract the most flavor, add them during cooking. When substituting dried herbs for fresh ones, a good rule of thumb is to use half the required amount.

* In a pinch, the garlic may still be used after the sprout is removed.

STAPLE UTENSILS

Contrary to what most kitchenware manufacturers would have you believe, the most important utensils for a kitchen are good, fresh ingredients and a little creativity. The following utensils installed in a minimally outfitted kitchen will allow you to make every recipe in this book.

10" non-stick (professional, if possible) sauté pan with lid.
The most important tool in my kitchen (see The $100 Kitchen Revolution).

3 gallon pot with lid.
Good for soups, pastas, and roof leaks during rainstorms.

Serrated (vegetable) knife.
I use one 6" serrated tomato knife for virtually everything I do.

6" Chef's knife.
Henckels is the Cadillac of these knives; any sharp knife will do.

Double bladed chopper.
Not essential, but great for The Rumanian eggplant purée, and the perfect tool for chunky guacamole.

Wood or plastic cutting board.
The best buys can be found at professional cooking supply stores.

Vegetable steamer.
The $5 variety is still the best.

12" Colander.
A must for pasta. Doubles as a lettuce drip drier.

Grater.
De rigueur for freshly grated parmesan cheese, ginger, nutmeg, etc. The four sided version is another $5 classic.

Garlic press.
The most frequently used utensil in my kitchen. Just like a mouse trap, the basic original remains the state of the art.

Mallet.
Required for flattening chicken.

Wooden bowl.
A Caesar salad's best friend (see The Art of the Salad).

Blender.
High tech versions are nice, but there is nothing my original '50s two speed Osterizer can't do.*

Corkscrew!

* Although I never personally have used one, I confess a certain small appreciation for the versatility of food processors, which can be helpful in puréeing foods to varying degrees of texture.

ETC...

THE $100 KITCHEN REVOLUTION

BUILDING A SIMPLE HERB GARDEN ($20)
(IT ONLY TAKES A LITTLE THYME.)

It is often said that food is the drug of the '90s. An herb garden provides the perfect opportunity to make use of the horticultural skills you cultivated back in the Haight-Ashbury days. Take a quick trip to the local nursery and purchase one or more of each of the following seedlings: basil, thyme, oregano, rosemary, and mint (usually $1 to $2 each). If you do not have an available window box or patch of garden, pick up a couple 10" plastic or clay pots and a bag of potting soil. Transplant the seedlings. When placed in direct sunlight and watered regularly, this collection of herbs will grow quickly. For seasonal climates, plant herbs in pots that can be brought inside during the winter months. Within a month, your instant herb garden will make a difference you can taste in your daily cooking. Simply clip off the leaves as you need them.

THE SECRET OF SAUTEING ($35)

Many of the dishes in this book are made in a sauté pan. This type of cooking is fast, and it allows you to see if you are burning the meal before it's too late (see Sauté Technique). I highly recommend a 10" Silver Stone pan, the professional chef's equivalent to Teflon, available at most restaurant supply stores. The non-stick coating allows you to reduce the amount of butter or oil required for sautéing, plus it's a breeze to clean. If you're feeling indulgent, spoil yourself with a rubber handle for an extra $5.

ART SUPPLIES ($40 - $80)

Plates are a chef's palette. Nothing facilitates the art of presentation better than an oversized (14") solid color plate. Pale yellow, turquoise, and white plates are especially effective as a foil for the colors in the food and garnishes you'll be using (see Presentation and Garnish sections for more details). These plates can be expensive (approximately $20 each), but two or four are all you need for most special occasion dinners. I have two of each color, enabling me to select the plates that work best with the colors of the food I'm cooking. If I'm cooking for four or six, the variety of plates lends a colorful, festive look to the table.

10 ENVIRONMENTALLY FRIENDLY THINGS YOU CAN DO FOR YOUR KITCHEN

SKIP THIS PAGE IF:

a) You have vowed to shoot the next person (or author) who champions "this year's cause" of environmental conservation or

b) You have already implemented your own environmentally friendly agenda

1) RECYCLE: With the increased awareness of recycling, depots are now far more plentiful and conveniently located. Separate and recycle paper and plastic bags, aluminum and tin cans, and glass and plastic bottles.

2) BUY RECYCLED GOODS: Slowly but surely, industry is catching up to the recycling phenomenon. Buying products such as recycled paper towels and napkins generates demand for recycled products, which in turn drives the whole recycling machine.

3) USE ENVIRONMENTALLY FRIENDLY CLEANERS: Biodegradeable dishwashing detergents and spray cleaners are now readily available in all health food stores and many grocery stores. This one is a no-brainer since these products achieve the same results as the similarly priced "unfriendly" ones they replace. Exhaust all options before using heavy duty drain cleaners.

4) USE WASHABLE RAGS: Keep a couple of rags and sponges in the kitchen and get into the habit of using them instead of paper towels whenever possible. When washing them, use a non-phosphorous environmentally friendly laundry detergent.

5) BUY BULK AND MINIMALLY PACKAGED PRODUCTS: Avoid unnecessarily elaborate packaging in favor of "smarter" minimal packaging. In addition to saving the excess packaging in the short run, you are increasing the demand for simpler packaging in the long run. This is the only barometer that most manufacturers really pay attention to.

6) COMPOST: Composting is like a low-tech science class experiment. It decomposes most kitchen and garden wastes in a specially designed bin, converting them into a rich, nutrient soil additive. For those who have the backyard space, composting serves three great purposes: it reduces the volume of garbage going to the dumps by up to 30 percent, it generates a healthy soil additive for your flower or vegetable garden which essentially takes the the minerals from your discarded food and returns them to the soil; it is an easy-to-understand concept for the children that demonstrates the fundamentals of recycling. (See Basics for a more detailed description of how to compost.)

7) USE FRESH VS. CANNED FOODS: Think fresh. Whenever possible, try to use fresh vs. canned, frozen, or pre-packaged fruits and vegetables. Not only will you eliminate packaging, but you are usually eating fresher, healthier, more flavorful foods with fewer preservatives.

8) ASK YOUR PRODUCE PERSON TO STOCK ORGANIC VEGETABLES: As demand increases for vegetables grown without the use of toxic chemical pesticides, they will evolve from their current status of specialty foods (with the accompanying price premium) into the mainstream of grocery supplies.

9) SUPPORT YOUR LOCAL FARMERS: Shop at farmer's markets.

10) SHARE YOUR AWARENESS WITH FRIENDS AND NEIGHBORS: Pool your resources and share your environmentally friendly discoveries. Even though it may seem "old hat" to you, the vast majority of people still haven't caught on.

PORTABLE PARKING METER

Time Indicator permanently set at 36 minutes

☆ Transforms any curb into a legal parking space

Lightweight Telescoping Stand for Convenient Trunk Storage

☆ Saves your time for cooking and your money for groceries

Suction Cup Base fits securely to any curb

BASICS

BASIC RECIPES

PESTO

(MAKES APPROXIMATELY 2 CUPS,
ENOUGH FOR SIX TO EIGHT SERVINGS.)
Very simple to make once you gather the
ingredients. If you are going to the trouble
of making pesto, make extra and freeze it.

INGREDIENTS
2 cups fresh basil leaves (lightly compressed together)
2 garlic cloves, *minced*
1/3 cup pine nuts or walnuts
1/2 tsp. black pepper
I cup olive oil
1/2 cup parmesan cheese (or 1/4 cup parmesan
+ 1/4 cup pecorino or romano)
1/2 tsp. salt
Juice of 1/2 lemon (optional)

(i) Mix all ingredients together in a blender or food
processor until smooth. (ii) Adding lemon juice will maintain
the color. (iii) Pesto will last in the refrigerator for I week
and in the freezer for I month, if covered with a thin
layer of oil and sealed tightly.

CLARIFYING BUTTER

The sole purpose of this exercise is to
create butter to sauté with. Normal, unclarified
butter burns and browns over high heat. Clarified
butter has a higher smoke point than normal butter
because the milk solids (which make butter burn at
high temperatures) are removed.

In a heavy sauce pan over low heat, melt desired
amount of butter (it's easier with at least 1/4 lb.) When
butter is fully melted, remove from heat and let stand
for 3 minutes. The butter should settle into three
layers: a frothy top, a clear yellow middle, and a milky
solid bottom. Begin by skimming or spooning the froth
off the top. Then carefully and slowly pour out the clear
middle layer into a bowl while retaining all of the
white solids in the pan. Discard froth and solids.
If necessary, repeat skimming process on remaining
contents in bowl. Clarified butter, tightly contained and
refrigerated, will last almost indefinitely.

BREAD CRUMBS

(MAKES APPROXIMATELY I CUP, ENOUGH
FOR RECIPES SERVING TWO TO FOUR
OR A FAMILY OF 6 BIRDS.)
The more flavorful the bread, the more
flavorful the bread crumbs (Logic 101).

INGREDIENTS
4 slices of very stale bread,* *cut or torn into I" pieces.*
Dried herbs, as desired (not required for
recipes in this book)

Place ingredients in a blender or food
processor and blend. (I prefer to leave mine much
coarser than store bought crumbs.)

Note: Blending bread crumbs can be a frustrating
experience because the bread tends to clog in the
bottom of the blender and requires frequent adjusting.
Don't let those stale little creatures psych you out.

* Dry out partially stale bread (talk about splitting
hairs) in an oven at 300 degrees for 15 minutes.

CROUTONS

(MAKES APPROXIMATELY I CUP, ENOUGH
FOR FOUR SALAD SERVINGS.)
The best croutons are made from thickly
sliced, slightly stale flavorful breads
(e.g., sourdough, Italian, and pumpernickel).

INGREDIENTS
4 slices of bread, *cut into approx. 3/4" cubes*
1/3 cup olive oil
I garlic clove, *minced* (optional)
I tsp. of any dried herbs: oregano, thyme,
basil, etc. (optional)

(i) Place bread cubes in a large bowl, add oil and
other ingredients. Toss until oil is absorbed.
Place on a cookie sheet or tin foil and bake in a
pre-heated oven at 350 degrees for approximately
25 minutes until browned. Turn once or twice
so that all sides brown evenly. (ii) If you plan to make
your own croutons it is a good habit to save the
ends of bread loaves in the freezer. (iii) I don't bother
seasoning croutons for my Caesar salad since the
dressing tends to overpower their flavoring.
(iv) Store in an airtight container.

ROASTING PINE NUTS

Roasting pine nuts accentuates their sweet flavor.

PAN METHOD

Over medium heat, melt 1 tsp. of butter for every
1/2 cup of pine nuts. Add nuts to pan and brown on
one side (approximately 3 minutes). Turn and brown
on other side (approximately 2 minutes). Remove
excess butter by drying nuts on a paper towel.

OVEN/TOASTER OVEN METHOD

Place desired amount of nuts on a piece of tin foil
and toast under pre-heated broiler until brown
(approximately 3 minutes). Turn and toast until brown
on other side (approximately 1 minute).

CHICKEN STOCK

**(MAKES APPROXIMATELY 8 CUPS,
ENOUGH FOR SOUP RECIPES
SERVING SIX TO EIGHT)**

There are many varieties of stock recipes. I
have chosen chicken stock because it goes well
with broccoli and carrot soup. Stock is easy to
make and does not have to be time consuming.
Once all of the ingredients have been assembled,
the stock can be left to simmer on the stove
unattended for several hours. I must admit, I have
never taken the time to make stock myself (this
recipe was supplied by my editor), but all my arm-
chair critics claim it makes a noticeable difference.

INGREDIENTS

3 lbs. chicken wings or backs, or a mixture of
wings, backs, necks, and giblets. Do not use livers.
16 cups of water
2 medium onions, *peeled and quartered*
2 carrots, *peeled and quartered*
2 bay leaves
10 parsley stems, *leaves removed*
1/2 tsp. black peppercorns
1/2 tsp. dried thyme

(i) Rinse chicken parts and add to a large pot. Add water,
ensuring that all of the chicken is covered. Bring water to
a boil, then reduce heat and simmer. Skim fat and foam
from surface. Add remaining ingredients to pot and let simmer
(without boiling) for 2 - 4 hours, skimming fat and foam
occasionally. Strain stock through a colander lined with
cheesecloth. Discard solids. (ii) Stock can be refrigerated for a
few days, or frozen in small portions or in ice cube trays,
for much longer. (iii) Remove layer of fat when reheating.

CAJUN SPICES

**(MAKES 6 TSP., ENOUGH FOR
RECIPES SERVING SIX)**
Laissez le bon temps rouler
(Let the good times roll)

INGREDIENTS

1/2 tsp. salt,
1/2 tsp. black pepper
1/2 tsp. cayenne pepper
1 tsp. onion powder
1 tsp. garlic powder
3/4 tsp. dried oregano
3/4 tsp. dried thyme
1/4 tsp. ground nutmeg
3/4 tsp. paprika

Mix all ingredients together.

BRUSCHETTA

(SERVES TWO)
A basic bruschetta recipe to be used in combination
with other foods from this book.**

INGREDIENTS

4 slices of crusty country-style or Italian bread,
thickly sliced (for baguettes, slice lengthwise)
1 clove of garlic, *cut in half*
1/4 cup of olive oil, (preferably
virgin or extra virgin)
1/8 tsp. salt
1/8 tsp. fresh ground black pepper
4 fresh basil leaves or 1 sprig of oregano,
chopped coarsely.

Grill bread over coals (ideally) or toast until
very brown. Immediately after removing
bread from toaster, rub garlic over entire
surface of one side. (This will not consume
the clove; use remainder in other cooking or
discard.) Pour oil lightly over entire surface
and sprinkle with salt, pepper, and herbs.

** When not adding other elements from the book to
your bruschetta, top with a finely chopped ripe tomato.
(But only do this if you can locate a "real" tomato.)

Random Notes

CLEANING LEEKS: Leeks are very hospitable to dirt and sand. The easiest way to clean leeks is to cut them as required by the recipe and then rinse them thoroughly in a strainer or colander.

CLEANING SPINACH: To avoid gritty spinach, rinse thoroughly. After you are positive that all the dirt and sand have been removed, rinse again.

PREPARING ASPARAGUS: The lower third of the asparagus spear can be a bit tough. To tenderize it, remove the outer layer with a carrot peeler.

STEAMING: Steaming vegetables requires a vegetable steamer. Place steamer in a small pot. Add water until the level comes up to the bottom of the steamer (approximately 1"). Bring water to a boil and then add vegetables. Cover securely with a lid and steam to desired degree of tenderness (usually 5 - 10 minutes depending on the amount and density of the vegetables).

STORING FRESH LEAFY HERBS: Wash herbs and remove stems. Place between damp paper towels, wrap in a plastic bag, and refrigerate.

BONING CHICKEN BREASTS: Using a small sharp knife, cut away any cartilage and excess skin. Insert knife between the breast bone and the meat and cut meat away from bone. When there is enough to grab, pull remaining breast away from bone (surreal cooking is not an exact science). To remove the white tendon that runs inside the small fillet, grasp the top end of the fillet with one hand and with your other hand pinch the protruding tip of the tendon between the backside of the knife blade and your thumb. Pull.

COOKING WITH WINE: The flavor of quality wine will reflect itself in your cooking. A good rule of thumb is to use wines to cook with that you would choose to drink (although not one you would serve if you just won the lottery). Many chefs suggest cooking with the same wine that you plan to serve with the meal. This is known as "cheater's food and wine pairing."

Pre-Production

After a hard day's work, sometimes even a half hour of cooking requires more energy than may be available. On these occasions, it's nice to just grab a few prepared ingredients from the refrigerator and toss together a satisfying meal in five or ten minutes. The home-made solution rests in the art of "pre-production." When time permits, take an hour or two to "set up" your meals for the week.

PRE-COOK: In the summer, fire up the BBQ (or take advantage of one already in use) and during the off season make the most of the oven and saute pan to pre-cook chicken breasts, whole garlic bulbs, sweet peppers, new potatoes, yams, Japanese eggplants, etc. Sprinkle them with olive oil, and some herbs, seal tightly and refrigerate. These can add instant appeal to salads, pastas, rice dishes, pizzas, omelets, etc., or be served collectively as an antipasto dish.

PRE-PACKAGE: Spend a few minutes cleaning and prepping lettuces, vegetables, fresh herbs, meats, etc. and re-package them in a ready-to-use form. (Clean and prepare, but do not pre-slice and dice fruits and vegetables, as they lose their flavor and natural vitamins.)

PREPARE: Prepare food that can be consumed as is, or quickly reheated, several days later. Rumanian eggplant, Italian black olive paste, and most soups can provide hearty nourishment for the entire week (and their flavors actually improve over time).

TRANSLATIONS

(FOR THE BENEFIT OF NON-FOODIES AND PEOPLE LIVING OUTSIDE NORTH AMERICA)

ANGEL HAIR PASTA: Also called spaghettini. Very thin spaghetti pasta.

BRUSCHETTA: A hearty Italian variation of garlic bread (see Basics).

CILANTRO: Also known as coriander (but not to be replaced with coriander seeds). Looks similar to parsley. Most people love it. One out of one hundred says it tastes like soap.

CLAMATO JUICE: A premixed blend of tomato juice and clam juice.

FENNEL: A celery-like vegetable that tastes like liquorice.

COUS COUS: A grain-like pasta.

FUSILLI PASTA: Pasta in the shape of a corkscrew.

HALF & HALF CREAM: 10.5% milkfat.

HEAVY CREAM: 36% milkfat.

ITALIAN PARSLEY: A leafier more robust variety of parsley.

PEPPER VODKA: Vodka infused with the flavor of hot peppers.

PINE NUTS: Also called pignoli. A tiny rich creamy nut.

POTATO: How people who do not live in Britain or one of its colonies spell potatoe.

PUREE: To chop finely in a blender or food processor into a thick paste.

RADICCHIO: A slightly bitter tasting, rich man's purple cabbage.

RESERVE: Cookingspeak for "Set aside for use later in the recipe."

SALADINI: A mixture of baby lettuce greens.

SAUTE: A method of cooking that employs a rounded frying pan (see The Art of Sautéing).

TAMARI SAUCE: An aged, richer version of soy sauce, made without wheat.

TOMATO: How people who do not live in Britain or one of its colonies spell tomatoe.

YAM: A variety of sweet potato. More orange in color and sweeter than common sweet potatoes.

ZEST: The thin outer layer of an orange, lemon, or lime peel, finely grated.

10 GIFT SUGGESTIONS FOR PEOPLE WHO LIKE TO COOK

Professional sauté pan (see $100 Kitchen Revolution) $35
Large dinner plates (see $100 Kitchen Revolution) $20 each
Ingredients for an herb garden (see $100 Kitchen Revolution) $20
Henckels (or comparable brand) 6" chef's chopping knife $50
Wooden salad bowl (see The Art of the Salad) $40 & up
Small braid of garlic $15
String of dried hot peppers $15
Multi-colored peppercorns and/or a clear plastic pepper grinder $5 - $25
A year's subscription to a food magazine $18
The Surreal Gourmet! (or its mail-order posters) $15 - $75

...AND 4 GIFTS NOT TO BUY

An apron with something foolish printed on it
Potholders in the shape of fish or lobster claws
The latest "better mousetrap" version of a corkscrew
An electric pepper grinder

CAUTION

EGGS: There is a new school of thought that claims eggs should never be consumed unless they are fully cooked throughout. More moderate thinkers believe that coddling an egg will kill most of the potentially harmful bacteria. I naively continue to use raw eggs in my Caesar salad and California carbonara. If you are at all concerned about the risk of raw egg consumption, *DO NOT MAKE THESE RECIPES*. To avoid most of the potential problems, coddle your eggs by placing them, in their shell, in boiling water for 40 seconds. Remove and use as directed.

CHICKEN: Poultry is particularly susceptible to contamination by salmonella bacteria which can cause serious food poisoning (not to mention ruining a carefully prepared meal). After handling chicken, wash hands, utensils, and cutting boards with soap and hot water to keep any bacteria from spreading to other foods. It is a good habit to cut poultry on a disposable surface such as wax paper to avoid any contact with cutting boards. Ensure that chicken is always properly refrigerated. Cook fresh chicken within two days of purchasing and frozen chicken (kept frozen) within four months. Frozen chicken must be fully thawed before cooking. Always cook chicken until all of the meat is cooked (i.e., no hint of pink remaining). Never take chances. If there is ever a hint that chicken has not been carefully stored, discard it.

PORK: To insure against bacteria, cook all forms of pork thoroughly until the juices run clear and there is no hint of pink remaining.

FLAMBEING: Not recommended for perpetually stoned rock musicians with big hair and lots of hairspray. For the rest of us pedestrians, always check to see where your fire extinguisher is, and that it is in operating condition before flambéing. Remove any flammable objects from the area.

DRINKING AND DRIVING: Don't.

COMPOSTING

(ADAPTED FROM AN ARTICLE BY CATHERINE DYER, CO-OWNER OF SEEDS ORGANIC GARDEN, L.A.)

GETTING STARTED: The first step in composting is getting into the habit of separating the appropriate kitchen waste and collecting it in a separate container.

THE COMPOST BIN: Prefabricated plastic compost bins are available at most home improvement stores. You can also build your own, using four used wood pallets or four posts with chicken wire stretched around them. The optimum area is one cubic yard. The bin should be set outside on soil and can be camouflaged with your favorite shrubbery.

WHAT TO COMPOST/HOW IT WORKS: Dried brown organic materials like leaves and dead plant matter are called carbon. Wet green organic materials like kitchen waste (e.g., fruit and vegetable remains), lawn clippings, and other garden wastes are called nitrogen. Equal volumes of both carbon and nitrogen materials layered alternately as thinly as possible (no more then 5 inches per layer) will create a hot chemical reaction that breaks down the materials. The compost should be misted with a hose as it is layered and can benefit from an occasional layer of garden soil or leftover compost. An occasional turning will also help aerate the pile and speed the process. Within approximately 6 months the bottom layers will yield a rich dark humus.

WHAT NOT TO COMPOST: Never use any meat scraps, dairy products, or any foods that have been saturated in oil. These items generate undesirable organisms in the pile and may also contain negative bacteria. Avoid poisonous plants like oleander and eucalyptus and walnut leaves which produce a growth inhibiting substance.

WHAT TO DO WITH FINISHED COMPOST: Finished compost is nutrient packed and has the added benefit of neutralizing the soil, whether too alkaline or too acid. Add it like a fertilizer around trees and shrubs, in your vegetable garden, rose garden, etc.

For more information see *Backyard Composting*, Harmonious Press.

SALMON WRAPPING

(for Grilled Salmon recipe)

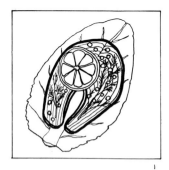  

1   2   3

Mail order address for dried chili pepper strands:
The Old Santa Fe Chili Co.
218 Old Santa Fe Trail
Santa Fe, N.M., U.S.A. 87501
Tel. (800) 950-0005

MUSIC TO COOK BY

(ALPHABETICAL ORDER BY ARTIST)

Academy of St. Martin-in-the-Fields, Conducted by Neville Marriner   *Bach, The Brandenburg Concertos*   Phillips
Bach's classic concertos. Neville Marriner's version gets my vote because he not only stopped to pick my mother up when she was hitchhiking back from
the Tanglewood Music Festival, but he got out of his car to open the door for her.

Chet Baker   *Let's Get Lost*   Novus/RCA
Chet Baker was the James Dean of trumpet players. I was introduced to his music by Bruce Weber's documentary of the same name. When he plays,
you melt, and when he sings, his voice is as smooth as his trumpet sound.

Bulgarian State Female Vocal Choir   *Le Mystère des Voix Bulgares*   Electra
Wafting, ethereal choral music. For Adventure Club members only.

Boozo Chavis   *Boozo Chavis*   Electra
Raw, swamp-crawling, toe-tappin', crayfish-shucking, accordian zydeco music from one of its authentic forefathers.

Jimmy Cliff   *The Harder They Come*   Mango
One of the classic reggae albums of all time. From the 1972 movie of the same name. Still sounds as smooth today as it did then. For something a little
tougher, spin Bob Marley or Sly and Robbie.

Leonard Cohen   *I'm Your Man*   Sony Music
Literary real life angst from the poet laureate of singer songwriters.

Bob Dylan   *Highway 61 Revisited*   Sony Music
Change your oil and hit the highway with this classic. When Dylan turned 50, many of the retrospective articles listed this
album as one of his best.

Ella Fitzgerald & Louis Armstrong   *Porgy and Bess*   Polygram
Louis and Ella in their prime. If you're bit by the bug, track down a "Best of" Louis Armstrong collection that includes the song "What a Wonderful World."

Gipsy Kings   *Gipsy Kings*   Electra
Real gypsy music from France.

Glen Gould   *Bach, The Goldberg Variations*   Sony Music
Piano playing as rich and as smooth as butter. The most popular album by the late tormented Canadian piano genius.

Bernard Herrmann   *Vertigo* (Alfred Hitchcock's soundtrack)   Mercury
After listening to this soundtrack, you'll need a double to calm your nerves.

Flaco Jimenez   *Ay Te Dejo en San Antonio*   Arhoolie Records
You'll smell the corn tortillas roasting as you play this Grammy Award winning Tex-Mex accordian dance music.

Nigel Kennedy   *Vivaldi's Four Seasons*   EMI
Britain's enfant terrible of the violin. I spent the better part of an evening with him. He really is bad to the bone.

k.d. lang   *Shadowland*   Sire
k.d., a notorious vegetarian, made me promise to list her under a vegetable recipe. One of the richest voices and most unique artists to emerge from the
'80s. There's never a dull moment with k.d. This particular album is a collection of classic ballads recorded with Patsy Cline's producer, Owen Bradly. Find
out why everyone from Madonna to Liza Minnelli are big fans. Also check out *Ingenue*.

Los Lobos   *La Pistola y el Corazón*   Warner Bros.
(The pistol and the heart) Los Lobos hit the spotlight with the La Bamba soundtrack. This accoustic collection of re-fashioned traditional Mexican folk
music brings the band back to their roots.

Lyle Lovett   *Pontiac*   Curb/MCA
One of my all-time favorite artists. All of his albums are brilliant. The wry Texan's music mixes country, folk, and swing. Go to his concerts, but not
to his barber.

Manteca   *Perfect Foot*   Nova/ Duke Street
Manteca is soca/pop/funkalypso band that will have you dancing, daiquiri in hand.

Van Morrison   *The Best of Van Morrison*   Mercury
A great collection of songs for anybody whose collection is lacking representation from this Irish singer extraordinaire. Morrison was partially responsible
for the selections on this album so they range from some of his more obscure songs to the classics you can sing along to. Of course, any Van Morrison
album from your collection will be a suitable replacement.

The Neville Brothers   *Yellow Moon*   A&M
Sweet sweet music. Producer extraordinaire, Daniel Lanois, brings out the best from this soulful New Orleans-based band.

Edith Piaf   *The Voice of the Sparrow (Best of Collection)*   Capitol
An instantly uplifting collection of music that will transform your home into a French cabaret.

Astor Piazzolla   *Tango: Zero Hour*   Pangaea/IRS
The great Argentinian accordion player's name is synonymous with the tango, still one of the most sensuous dances in the world. According to someone
who has recorded with him, this is Astor's favorite album and fortunately one of the most readily available from his vast catalogue.

Elvis Presley   *The Sun Sessions*   RCA
A compilation of hits from Elvis's formative years on the Sun Records label. Elvis at his innocent best. Includes outtakes and alternate takes.

Louis Prima   *Zuma*   Rhino
Fifties big band jazz-swing-early rock n' roll. Happy happy music.

Nino Rota   *Music from the Films of Fellini*   ITM
Music from Italian director Federico Fellini's classic films.

Jane Siberry   *Bound by the Beauty*   Reprise
After managing and traveling the world with Jane for ten years, I am still a fan. Begin with this album and then graduate to the rest of her catalogue. I have
included Jane's music with my garlic recipe because of the garlic-scented memories she evokes. While on tour we would frequently coerce restauranteurs
into baking us garlic bulbs which we would devour on the tour bus after the show. Note: If you lived on a bus for months at a time surrounded by 12
garlic-crazed musicians, you too would begin to have halucinatory visions of floating carrots.

Frank Sinatra   *Songs for Swingin' Lovers*   Capitol
Sinatra can still outsing anyone. Don't be put off by the once hip title. Try it, or either of the boxed sets now available. You'd be surprised how many
people haven't rediscovered these gems. For the second round of drinks, play some old Dean Martin, the man whose name is synonymous with martinis.

Various artists   *Puccini's Greatest Hits*   Sony Music
Irresistible opera music that will appeal to the uninitiated and the connoisseur.

Various artists   *Legends of Guitar, Surf Vol. 1*   Rhino
Do not be put off by the title. This is a great collection of original '60s guitar surf tunes. Grab your board, or your sauté pan and hang 10.

Tom Waits   *Frank's Wild Years*   Island
How does one describe the music of a guy who sings through a megaphone and borrows from vaudeville, burlesque, and the Tin Pan Alley? While listening
to this album, it's easy to picture Waits at the piano in Hollywood's seedy Tropicana Hotel where he held his fabled residency.

WINE JOURNAL

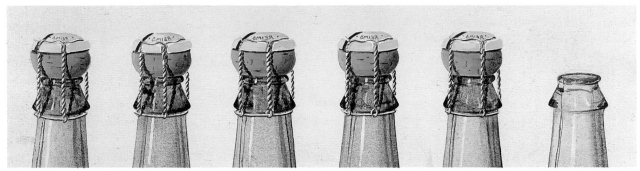

Name	Year	Country	Price	Comments - Winning combinations

QUIRKODEX

Murphy's Law of cooking states: "Whatever you intend to serve is exactly what at least one of your guests can't eat, is allergic to, or had a bad experience with as a child." The probability of this occurrence increases exponentially in relation to the degree of difficulty of the dish or the rarity of the ingredient in question.

This page is designed to allow you to keep track of the dietary quirks of your dinner guests. Write on it: this is not a library book!

Name	Foods they don't eat	Favorite foods	Beverage(s) of choice

SPECIAL THANKS TO MY KITCHEN CABINET

Alison Emilio: for the farfetched suggestion that I should write a cookbook.
Dick Kaiser: for the excellent photography, all of the brainstorming, and understanding that the "five shooting days" were measured on my surreal calender.
Matt Zimbel (fellow professional generalist and kindred spirit): for remaining enthusiastic after so many calls and faxes. Hey Matt, first I'll take Manhattan....
Mark Collis (professional chef): for sharing a few of his trade secrets.
Jane Siberry: for trading hats and being so supportive.
Meesha "I'll be the one holding a carrot at the Burbank airport loading zone" **Halm:** for "getting it."
Gina Stepaniuk: for being Gina.
Nion McEvoy: for allowing me to stop at #1 on my wish list of publishers.

Charlotte & everyone at Chronicle Books, Kate Burns, Susan Grode, Melanie Ciccone, Kevin Reagan, Marjorie Skouras, Edgar Moss & Jacki Fitzgibbon, Margaret Johnstone, Christopher Bird, Quincy Houghton, Debbie Jow, Sarah Blumer, Maureen & Pat Doherty, Corey & Erika, Karen Gordon, Shirley Stewart, Sarah Burns, Sandy Gleysteen, Norman Perry, Robert Phillips, H"bh"VP, Candice Bowes, Chris Douridas, Veronique Vial, Guy & Nathalie, Rosalie Goldstein, Mark & Ami, Isabell Mejias, Dennis Kightley, Janis Mackintosh, Rush Copy – Hollywood, Libby Stone for letting me lean over the fence and swipe grapefruits, Ellen Rose – The Cook's Library, Rachael Fratto – Utensils, all of my friends who have shared these meals with me...and a tip of the bowler hat to René Magritte.

ORIGINAL LIMITED EDITION PRINTS

SIGNED, SURREALED & DELIVERED

To order limited edition prints of the Caesar Salad (pg. 18) or Orange Twist Blueprint (pg. 71) write:
The Surreal Gourmet, P.O. Box 2961, Hollywood, CA 90078-2961 USA